Green **Walls** Green **Roofs**

Green **Walls** Green **Roofs**

Designing sustainable architecture

images
Publishing

Published in Australia in 2014 by
The Images Publishing Group Pty Ltd
ABN 89 059 734 431
6 Bastow Place, Mulgrave, Victoria 3170, Australia
Tel: +61 3 9561 5544 Fax: +61 3 9561 4860
books@imagespublishing.com
www.imagespublishing.com

National Library of Australia Cataloguing-in-Publication entry:

Title:	Green Walls Green Roofs / Gina Tsarouhas
ISBN:	9781864705522 (hardback)
Notes:	Includes index.
Subjects:	Green roofs (Gardening)
	Wall gardens.
	Vertical gardening.
	Architecture--Details.
Edited by:	Gina Tsarouhas
Dewey Number:	635.9671

Designed by Rod Gilbert, The Graphic Image Studio Pty Ltd, Mulgrave, Australia
www.tgis.com.au

Pre-publishing services by Mission Productions Limited, Hong Kong
Printed on 140gsm Dodong Woodfree by Everbest Printing Co. Ltd., in Hong Kong/China

IMAGES has included on its website a page for special notices in relation to this and our
other publications. Please visit www.imagespublishing.com.

CONTENTS

FOREWORD

by Matthew Dillon

Matthew has an architectural background encompassing sustainable building design, landscape design and sculpture. He has been focused on green infrastructure advocacy since 2007 speaking at international conferences, consulting to the City of Sydney and lobbying government for industry incentives and policy change. He is principal consultant with Verdant Solutions Australia; a board member with the World Green Infrastructure Network; and president of Green Roofs Australasia, the peak body for promoting green infrastructure.

This foreword encourages the incorporation of green infrastructure into the urban fabric of our towns and cities as one solution towards a sustainable future with nature. The examples chosen for this book represent a rapidly expanding industry, which has the potential to provide profound environmental, socio-cultural and economical benefits to urban populations and a blueprint for developing our built environment with nature. This book exemplifies the notion that we can replace the landscape covered by a building footprint with a green roof or a living wall, as a responsible, sustainable compromise with nature.

Beyond the aesthetic beauty of the examples presented, setting out a case for growing plants on our buildings is also an important part of this book. I share a view with many associated in urban planning, architecture and landscape architecture – that a holistic strategy for built environment design can enhance the functionality of urban ecosystems by positively contributing to air/water quality, energy use and biodiversity while also providing new natural habitats, stormwater management and carbon sinks. This is currently referred to as green infrastructure for the built environment and includes living walls, green roofs, urban forests, canopy trees, street swales, rain gardens and revegetation.

These practices provide multifunctional benefits, which include socio-cultural benefits to rising urban population density. Research has determined that an increased interaction with plants will improve our physical and mental health, improve well being, and lift cognitive ability for adults, especially in work environments dominated by partition walls and artificial lighting.

I was overjoyed to be present with Mark Paul (founder of The Greenwall Company) and the students of Mosman Primary recently when we worked with the children to plant in recycled plastic drink bottles and create a beautiful living wall in their playground (see Bottling the Idea, p54). Such projects are testament to qualitative research in the USA, which concluded that plants improve children's educational performance, happiness and well being. Trial green infrastructure projects in low-income, high-crime neighbourhoods have shown a reduction in crime and domestic violence, reinforcing the need to support a transition from grey to green. The practice of greening cities is rapidly expanding, however, so too is the practice of unsustainable grey infrastructure. Concrete highways dissect our landscape and ecosystems connecting expansive urban sprawl; concrete is laid over the landscape; trees are cleared and buildings erected.

As a counter to this unsustainable urban planning there is now a strong argument for transitional change towards green cities that 'mimic' natural ecosystems, based on new quantifiable and qualifiable data. Globally there is a green revolution taking place in city lanes, streets and on buildings through the implementation of community roof gardens, urban farming, guerrilla landscaping, living walls, green roofs, street canopy planting, swales, rain gardens, water harvesting, water filtration and recycling. This book celebrates the spirit of this urban green revolution.

The case studies outlined are indicative of what can become mainstream living architecture or 'vegitecture', which will also require a determination and conviction from our government leaders and decision makers to implement new policy, finance new research, provide industry incentives and maintain a sustainable, resilient strategy to secure our ecosystems for future generations.

Significant components of green infrastructure are green roofs and living walls, which are vegetated systems requiring professional specifications and design to grow successfully in site specific micro- and macro-climatic conditions. Urban density, real estate prices and construction costs have impacted on ground-level landscaping, shifting focus to roof and façade space for new greening.

The use of green roofs is not new and first appeared in the ancient Roman and Persian civilisations of 8th century BC, notably the Hanging Gardens of Babylon, the Euphrates and the Tigris valleys. Ornamental gardens and grass roofs have since been a feature of vernacular architecture for centuries throughout Scandinavia and Kurdistan, providing insulation during summer and winter temperature extremes. By the 1850s developments in modern building materials and the use of concrete as a flat roofing material saw the introduction of extensive roof greening in Europe and America from innovative architects like Gropius in Cologne, Le Corbusier in Germany and Frank Lloyd Wright in Chicago. Although influential architects of their time, the practice was never fully embraced by mainstream until Friedensreich Hundertwasser epitomised a counter-culture resurgence with a building holding 900 tons of soil and 250 trees and various shrubs in Vienna. From here it was the German-speaking nations that developed what we now consider the modern green roof. From 1960–70 there were many projects in Germany and Switzerland that experimented with new innovative ways of using vegetated systems on building roofs. During the 1980s the problems of water- and root-penetration were solved and it was then obvious to German visionaries who could imagine how future cities could

be planned. Since the 1950s Germany has led the world with research on green roofing, policy, urban planning and installations. There is no doubt that the lightweight technology now available is a result of Germany's research and innovation with plants.

Most countries now have an awareness about the potential benefits for reducing the impacts of the Urban Heat Island Effect; improving water and air quality; mitigating noise pollution; improving building energy efficiency; providing more green amenity spaces for urban density projects; providing habitat for flora and fauna; growing food on urban roof-top farms and improving our general well being, health and social fabric. Significant positive impacts can be achieved with widespread green roofs and living walls that connect to urban hinterlands via concentrated green zones at nodal points along urban green corridors. Alternatively, the occupants of a single residence can benefit from a green roof and living walls in the same way as an entire city. Multiply the plants and we multiply the benefits for a sustainable future.

It seems logical that if we cover the landscape footprint with concrete then we should replace it with a green roof connected to a vertical living wall back to earth. Think again about flying over urban sprawl and seeing only green. Think again after reading this book.

COMMERCIAL CONFIDENCE

BREATHING IN NATURE

The **Goodman NZ office**, on the main street in Auckland, New Zealand, boasts four floor-to-ceiling green walls, including a two-storey-tall wall in the foyer.

Opaque glass panels silhouette the green walls, so occupants in the project space behind can also enjoy the green ambience. 'The green walls create a lovely environment to work in and are often complimented by visitors,' says the office manager at Goodman.

Natural Habitats focused on two key criteria when selecting plants for this project: assessing the level of lighting available in the building and ensuring good access for people, thus it opted for low-light tropical plants that would grow in a relatively narrow depth out from the wall. The green walls create an oxygenated office environment.

Photography supplied by Natural Habitats Ltd

This luscious ensemble of thriving plants is found 28 levels up in Auckland's city centre

CONNECTING WITH THE OUTSIDE WORLD

SOUTHERN CROSS HEALTH SOCIETY RECEPTION →
WESTPAC RECEPTION ←

The **Britomart East Complex** green wall in Auckland was designed by **Natural Habitats** to achieve a New Zealand Green Building Council five-star rating. The living walls line the east- and west-end walls and integrate seamlessly into the building fabric. The introduction of these vertical gardens has improved air quality and acoustics, providing office occupants a sense of connection with the natural environment.

The green walls feature a custom-designed planting palette that incorporates a combination of native and exotic species chosen for their low light and maintenance requirements. The overall composition was influenced by the shadows that fall on the wall during the day, with repetition of planting patterns loosely referencing those found in traditional Maori carvings.

The wall consists of 60 custom-made panels, which had been grown off-site for several months prior to installation, providing a mature plant density. At 130 square metres (1399 square feet) it's currently the largest green wall in New Zealand.

As the walls are only 120mm deep, the lightweight inert medium (as opposed to soil), can be easily fixed into the atrium's existing stud pattern. This was installed using a building maintenance unit and abseiling equipment.

Photography supplied by Natural Habitats Ltd

The repetition of planting patterns loosely references traditional Maori carvings

This project involved improvements to the multistorey atrium space and the replacement of an unattractive façade fronting most of the offices at the A&A building at **158 Cecil St**, Singapore. Designed and conceptualised by the architects from **AgFacadesign**, the inspiration came from the grand spaces of Notre Dame and Gothic architecture, based on the concept of a 'hanging garden by day and a glowing lantern by night'.

To achieve an indoor-outdoor environment, a ventilated layered glass façade was developed by **G FAÇADESIGN Pte Ltd** to provide natural ventilation, while still allowing the natural elements to enter to support plant growth. All unsightly existing surfaces and structural elements, such as the auto irrigation system, were carefully integrated with the plants (with help from landscape designers **Tierra Design [S] Pte Ltd**) to enrich the architecture and enliven the atrium-interior spaces.

By day, the hanging garden is a calm and soothing environment. By night, the building transforms into a glowing green lantern.

Photography by AgFacadesign

Structural elements were transformed into features to enhance the spatial quality of the hanging garden

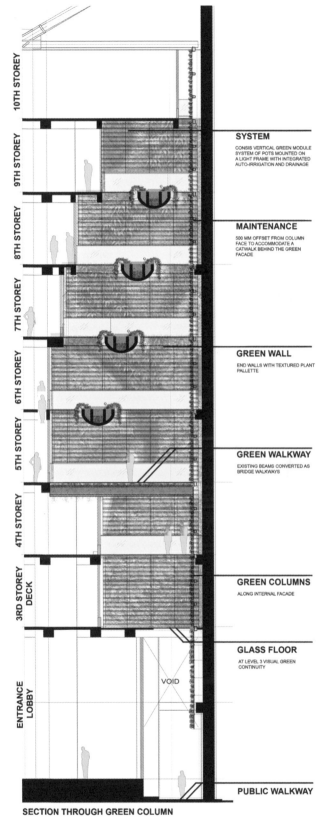

10TH STOREY

9TH STOREY

SYSTEM

CONSIS VERTICAL GREEN MODULE SYSTEM OF POTS MOUNTED ON A LIGHT FRAME WITH INTEGRATED AUTO-IRRIGATION AND DRAINAGE

8TH STOREY

MAINTENANCE

500 MM OFFSET FROM COLUMN FACE TO ACCOMMODATE A CATWALK BEHIND THE GREEN FAÇADE

7TH STOREY

6TH STOREY

GREEN WALL

END WALLS WITH TEXTURED PLANT PALLETTE

5TH STOREY

GREEN WALKWAY

EXISTING BEAMS CONVERTED AS BRIDGE WALKWAYS

4TH STOREY

3RD STOREY DECK

GREEN COLUMNS

ALONG INTERNAL FAÇADE

GLASS FLOOR

AT LEVEL 3 VISUAL GREEN CONTINUITY

ENTRANCE LOBBY

VOID

PUBLIC WALKWAY

SECTION THROUGH GREEN COLUMN

FORMING AN ECOLOGICAL NEXUS

Solaris is a research and office building located at the 1-north business park of central Singapore. The building is a prototype ecodesign of **T. R. Hamzah & Yeang Sdn. Bhd** (as the architect-of-design) with **CPG Consultants** (as the architect-of-record) and has been certified BCA Green Mark Platinum, the highest possible green certification granted by Singapore's BCA's sustainable building benchmark.

Solaris stands as a demonstration of the possibilities inherent in an ecological approach to building design. The project comprises two tower blocks separated by a grand, glazed and naturally ventilated central atrium, with automated glass louvres above, and which is linked by a series of sky bridges that span the atrium at upper floors. The building has become a vibrant focal point for the 1-north community through its open interactive spaces, sky courts and its unique continuous spiral landscaped ramps that form an extension of the 1-north Park across the street. The landscaped ramp enables an ecological nexus from the basement to the upper floors, linking together a stepped sequence of roof gardens with sky terraces that punctuate the corners of building's façade.

Its key feature is the uninterrupted 1.5-kilometre-long (0.93-mile-long) ecological 'vertical linear park' that connects the vegetation at ground level and an 'ecocell' at the basement with the cascading sequence of roof gardens at the building's highest levels. Pedestrian circulation in the spiral, landscaped ramp is achieved via a parallel pathway, which also allows access for servicing the continuous planters. The landscaped pathway, as a 'park' within a building, stretches all the way from the ground plane to the uppermost roof area. The vegetated ramp climbs one floor at every façade, and where it reaches a corner of the building it opens access out into a large terrace. Together, these features enable an open and greener way of life for the office occupants, beyond the otherwise conventional hermetically sealed office environment.

The continuity of the landscaping is a key component of the project's ecological design concept: it allows for fluid connectivity of selected flora and fauna between all vegetated areas within the building, enhancing the locality's biodiversity and overall health of the habitats. The ramp – with its deep overhangs and large concentrations of shade plants – is part of the project's strategy for the ambient cooling of the building's façade.

An experimental diagonal solar-shaft cuts through the upper floors of Tower A allows daylight to penetrate deep into the building's interiors. Internal lighting operates on a system of sensors, which reduces energy use by automatically turning off lights when adequate daylight is available. Landscaped terraces within the solar-shaft bring added internal transitional spaces to the office floors and provide views from street level up into the building.

Singapore lies along the equator with the sun-path almost exactly east–west. Façade studies analysing the solar-path determined the shape and depth of the sunshade louvres, which also double as light-shelves. In conjunction with the spiral landscaped ramp, sky gardens, and deep overhangs, the sunshade louvres also assist in establishing comfortable micro-climates in habitable spaces along the edge internal spaces of the building floors.

The building's vertical landscaping acts as a thermal buffer. Besides this, it also provides areas for relaxation and small event spaces. The extensive roof gardens allow building's occupants to interact with nature and enjoy views of the treetops of the adjacent one-North Park.

The building's extensive landscaping is irrigated via a water management system consisting of a rainwater harvesting and recycling system where the rainwater is collected from the downpipes at the landscaped ramp's perimeter and from the roof of Tower B, via a siphonic drainage system. It is stored in rooftop tanks and at the lowest basement level, which also collects the condensate from the air-conditioning system. The integrated system helps maintain organic nutrient levels throughout the irrigation cycle.

Photography by Robert Such, CPG Consult

The building's vegetated areas are irrigated almost exclusively via harvested rainwater

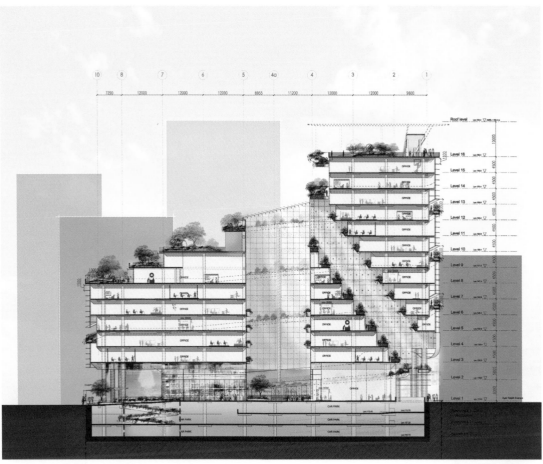

Designed by **William McDonough + Partners**, this building in Hoofddorp, The Netherlands, exemplifies the latest in sustainable thinking. **B/S/H Inspiration House** features a full-height, four-storey atrium with an indoor/outdoor living green wall and a BIPV roof that maximises energy and daylight. High efficiency LED lighting, daylight dimming sensors and rooftop solar panels result in integrated systems that perform 53% above conventional building standards, and are 39% more efficient than current code-compliant buildings.

The specification process favoured materials that are beneficial to human health, ecological health and are designed for technical and/or biological cycles. The building is constructed using a light-weight prefabricated steel frame to reduce the amount of weight. A unitised glass and aluminum panel cladding also reduced the amount of material required for construction. Other material content considerations included recyclable/recycled materials, salvaged materials, locally available and/or rapidly renewable materials and certified wood. When possible, products that have been assessed and certified through the Cradle to Cradle^{CM} Products Program are specified; this program is recognised as the highest standard for safe and healthy products.

The structure's interior spaces are designed to encourage occupant well-being through individual user controls, fresh air and sunlight, and materials assessments ensure that safe and healthy products are used throughout the building. Office spaces on the two top floors are designed according to the innovative 'new way of working' principle: the space comprises zones that feature alternative workplaces and flexible use of furniture. Each floor features a hub, where all the community functions such as meeting rooms, coffee corners, concentration spots, and informal working and meeting areas are clustered.

Throughout the various workspaces and showrooms there is contact with green, both horizontally and vertically. The green wall uses limited water, with air-purifying plants and overlapping panels that create a watertight system. The building's roof surfaces feature Xeroflor green roofs and roof garden systems, which include a rainwater catchment basin that filters and stores grey water for reuse.

Photography: courtesy D/Dock Amsterdam; ©Foppe Schut, courtesy D/Dock Amsterdam; ©HansOostrom Photography; ©IBB, courtesy William McDonough + Partners; and ©William McDonough + Partners

Thinking of buildings like trees — able to produce energy, create habitat, cleanse and store rainwater

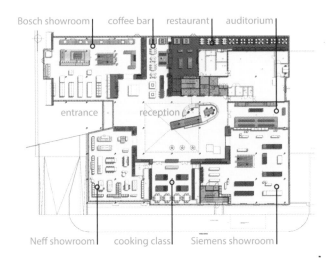

Bosch showroom · coffee bar · restaurant · auditorium

entrance · reception

Neff showroom · cooking class · Siemens showroom

MERGING NATURE
& BUILDING

The signature patient tower building – with its gently curving form – figuratively opens its arms to welcome patients. A vertical garden at the center of the south façade overlooks the extensive landscaped roof and garden terraces – designed with **Spurlock Poirier Landscape Architects** – above the two-storey diagnostic and treatment wing. The conservatory element is repeated at the eastern and wesern ends to reinforce the garden hospital concept. Site planning, landscaping, non-institutional architectural expression, and materials selection are all strongly influenced by the desire to merge nature and building, with each aspect informing the other to create a unified whole.

The surgical wing's green roof, planted with drought-tolerant succulents, provides a connection to nature for patients in the nursing tower and is integrated into the building's structural and mechanical performance. There are wonderful views from the nursing tower over the site to distant hills and mountains, and the green roof provides a foreground landscape. The roof also contributes to energy efficiency by reducing ground reflectance and solar heat gain in the tower's interiors and is integrated into the storm-water management system. Biodegradable biotray technology has been used to retain the steep slope of the green roof. Outdoor courts cut into the two-

CO Architects was charged with developing a facility for the **Palomar Medical Center** as the 'hospital of the future'. The design concept was for a functional and flexible vertical garden hospital, set within a campus configuration, located on a greenfield site in California, USA.

storey wing, bringing natural light to the functionally determined deep-floor plates.

Conservatory gardens are located at the center and at both ends of each patient floor. In addition to bringing landscaped gardens to all the inhabitants of the vertical building, they also provide an additional layer of solar protection for the fully glazed adjoining public spaces. The patient tower is oriented to minimise east/west exposures in its arid, inland valley context and is designed to take maximum advantage of daylight.

A perforated metal screen system on the south façade provides shade to patient rooms while allowing maximum views and natural light. The screen unifies the building's projecting elements and consists of two components: a second skin that sits parallel to the curtain-wall enclosure, and horizontal louvres that address summer sun angles. Where the screens extend to the garden terraces, they serve as wind protection for the high-rise outdoor spaces. Other energy-efficient measures at the medical centre include vigorous energy management systems, capture and reuse of waste heat, efficient lighting strategies, daylight controls, variable air-volume handling, building commissioning and the careful selection of energy-saving medical equipment.

Photography by Tom Bonner

The undulating roof creates interesting forms with different plant types

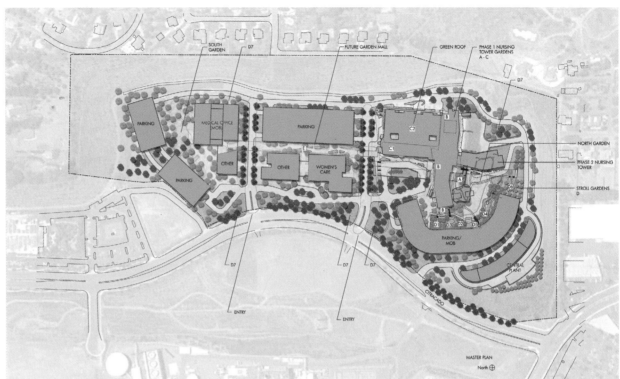

The largest living plant wall in New Zealand

The **Novotel Auckland Airport** was designed to combine New Zealand's distinctive cultural heritage with modern architecture. The green wall was designed, built and installed by **Natural Habitats** to complement the hotel's distinctive New Zealand ecodesign theme and act as a textural backdrop and focus for the bar area.

The two-storey-high swathe of green that envelops the bar from floor to ceiling features an array of native New Zealand flora. The wall helps to improve the bar's indoor air quality by removing air pollutants and raising humidity levels. The 60 square meters (645 square feet) of vertical vegetation provides both visual interest and environmental benefits, creating a more comfortable environment in which to work and relax.

Photography supplied by Natural Habitats Ltd

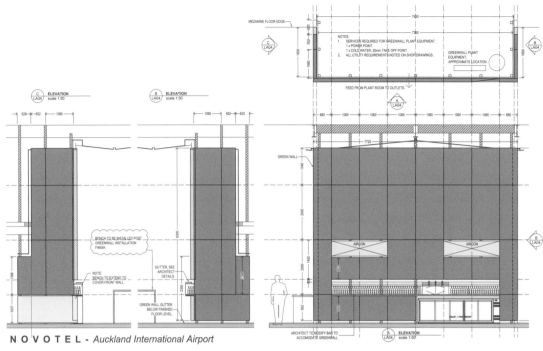

NOTES:
1. SERVICES REQUIRED FOR GREENWALL PLANT EQUIPMENT.
   1 x POWER POINT.
   1 x COLD WATER, 20mm TAKE OFF POINT.
2. ALL UTILITY REQUIREMENTS NOTED ON SHOP DRAWINGS.

GREENWALL PLANT EQUIPMENT, APPROXIMATE LOCATION.

FEED FROM PLANT ROOM TO OUTLETS

MEZANINE FLOOR EDGE

GREEN WALL.

C ELEVATION LA04 scale 1:50

B ELEVATION LA04 scale 1:50

A ELEVATION LA04 scale 1:50

BENCH TO BE INSTALLED POST GREENWALL INSTALLATION FINISH.

NOTE: BENCH TO EXTEND TO COVER FRONT WALL.

GUTTER, SEE ARCHITECT DETAILS.

GREEN WALL GUTTER BELOW FINISHED FLOOR LEVEL.

ARCHITECT TO MODIFY BAR TO ACCOMODATE GREENWALL

AIRCON   AIRCON

N O V O T E L - *Auckland International Airport*

STEPPING UP
TO NEW HEIGHTS

Australia's first green wall developer Mark Paul, founder and director of **The Greenwall Company**, has completed work on one of the tallest green walls in Australia. Spanning 22 floors of an **office in Melbourne**, each floor has its own unique planting make-up, specifically designed to maximise varying angles and lighting.

The building at Exhibition St is a refit of an existing building. It aims to be best practice in sustainability and energy efficiency through the design and installation of a state of the art trigeneration plant.

The Cogent Trigeneration Plant delivers heating and cooling for the building's air-conditioning system. It also provides low CO_2 emissions-density electricity when compared to the grid. This helps reduce the company's carbon footprint.

The wall forms a continuous green spine down the core of the building; it's a green lung and wild place for office staff to traverse while using the stairs between the floors.

As well as providing an instant, textural green solution to the architectural façade of the office environment, additional benefits of the green wall include thermal insulation, improved air quality, reduced noise and increased acoustics.

The Greenwall Company builds its walls from 94 percent of recyclable materials that would otherwise be destined for Australian landfill, taking the benefits of its green walls beyond just their aesthetic appeal.

Mark states: 'My goal is to reclaim the built environment, preserving biodiversity, recycling landfill waste and water waste resulting in much more than the sum of its original components. This project takes us one step closer to achieving this goal.'

Photography: courtesy of www.greenwall.com.au

The greenery is literally a living skin

EDUCATIONAL ENERGY & CULTURE

The roof of the **Native Child and Family Services Toronto** building in Ontario, Canada, has been converted to provide Urban Aboriginal with access to nature through cultural grounds, rituals and customs, and to crown the building with greenery. The green roof is used for recreational space for children, staff and clients, and ceremonies, including drumming and circle sessions.

A sacred medicine garden (planted with sweet grass, cedars, sage and tobacco) and a three-sisters garden (planted with corn, beans and squash) support cultural heritage and environmental awareness. A lush sampling of indigenous specimens from the Great Lakes region, including coniferous and sumac trees, wildflowers, grasses, herbs and agricultural plants, surround grass berm 'teaching hills', a

fire pit with stump seating and a dome-shaped healing lodge. The healing lodge's steel ribs, clad in rusted Corten steel and lined with scented cedar, signify branches and skins. A gas heat source is used to create a rooftop fire pit that meets fire codes.

Water trickles from a low fountain, introducing soothing natural sounds. Vines make the garden apparent from street level; they will cover the fencing to further enhance the natural experience from the rooftop, protect it from the city's noise and pollution, and further distinguish the building from its neighbours.

LGA Architectural Partners have shaped the space by considerations of sustainability: longevity, ease of maintenance and an informed selection of native species that will withstand harsh urban conditions with minimal water. The materials are locally sourced and the plants are watered with collected rainwater.

The green roof increases the site's useable outdoor space by 642 square metres (6,910 feet). Its thick membrane will likely extend the roof's lifespan by two to three times that of a conventional roof; it also provides additional insulation for the building, reducing heating and cooling costs.

Photography by Ben Rahn / A-Frame Inc.

A contemporary iteration of a healing lodge presents aboriginals with the only opportunity to participate in sweat rituals, without having to leave the city

BOTTLING THE IDEA

This project was created by **The Greenwall Company** and has been designed by company founder Mark Paul to reclaim the built environment and to educate students on the importance of recycling and creating natural habitats.

The **PET Bottle Greenwall Project** idea was developed and inspired by Mark's collaborative work with his Brazilian counterpart in Rio de Janeiro's favelas (shanty towns). The outcomes there were dramatic with long-lasting impacts for the residences of that very hostile urban environment.

This green wall is a soil-less vertical garden grown on the surface of a built structure and is designed to mimic the growing conditions found where green walls occur in nature, creating a habitat for small animals and insects. Plants on a green wall live without soil using many adapted strategies to survive poor nutrition, exposed conditions and seasonal drought. In the wild, plants colonise only those rocks and trees that provide adequate growing conditions: aspect, light, air movement, water and nutrients.

The immediate benefits of a bottle green wall are firstly its incredible beauty, however the wall also helps to insulate sound, deflect heat and provide a tranquil effect. Importantly, maintenance of a wall of this size, measuring 5 metres by 2 metres (16 feet, 4 inches by 6 feet, 4 inches), will only require the equivalent of 10 showers of recycled water over a one-year period. The wall utilises 600 PET bottles and other inorganic media that is greatly dependent on the properties of plastics to generate plant life.

Owned by the students, this project has proved to have a powerful effect at a local level and provides a fun learning experience; it also helps to instill intrinsic environmental values in the next generation.

Photography courtesy of www.greenwall.com.au

The project encourages students to proactively engage and participate in every step of the green wall's creation

BUILDING UP THE LAYERS

The **TU Library** of the University of Technology in Delft, in the Netherlands, was designed as an extension of the surrounding landscape. Like a wedge the building seems to be pushed below the lawn area, which is often used by the students for sitting or sunbathing during the summer time.

Unfortunately, after little more than ten years of use, significant deficiencies appeared at the roof and it had to be subjected to an overall refurbishment.

Mastum BV installed a pressure-resistant thermal insulation made of foam glass, as well as a new bituminous waterproofing with a top layer of root-resistant EPDM. The landscaping contractor, **Van der Tol BV**, chose a green roof Build-up so that it resists even the highest mechanical demands and is based on the solid drainage and protection layer.

Elastodrain® EL 202, which the System Build-up is based on, was covered by a system filter and then by the system substrate. In this case only 100 mm to 120 mm (4 inches to 4.7 inches) of substrate had to be enough for the lawn to achieve a reduction in weight compared to the initial Build-up with 200 mm (7.9 inches) of substrate depth. In hindsight this initial solution turned out to be too heavy for the roof construction. This project was made including a unique 10-year insurance backed warranty.

Photography by ZinCo/Van der Tol

The 13° sloped roof will remain perfectly protected

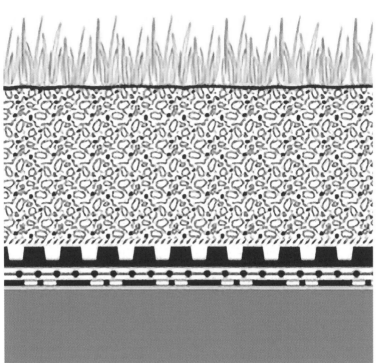

Plant layer 'Lawn'

System Substrate 'Lawn'

Filter Sheet TG

Elastodrain® EL 202

Roof construction with root-resistant waterproofing

In an over-a-century-old school, a new educational environment with a refreshed image and latest technology has been added. Architects **Tzannes Associates** have incorporated green technology into the façade of the building, designed for **Our Lady of Mercy College** at Parramatta, near Sydney, Australia, creating calm interior spaces suffused with natural light.

The building is characterised by a 60-metre-long (197 feet) two-storied arcaded green screen. The library is the main room of the new building and occupies the entire middle floor. The open floor plan allows a variety of learning experiences with transparent quiet rooms for small group study, areas that can be occupied by a class and comfortable furniture for individual

learning. The books surround the room inviting browsing and freeing up area from the traditional stack arrangement. The bookshelves make a place for display and above these large continuous windows open onto the two-storey steel-columned arcade with mesh covered with Star Jasmine and Bower of Beauty. The white and pink flowers are on alternate bays and together with the green leaves they suffuse the interior of the library with natural light.

The vines are supported on two gauges of stainless steel mesh trellis chosen to suit each of the plant types. This reinforces the alternating pattern of the structural bays.

The eastern part of the building that contains the learning areas is a columned pavilion fully glazed on three sides. The ground floor is set behind a curved concrete arcade forming a dignified entry. The arcade supports large precast concrete planters with inbuilt irrigation. On the upper floor the roof lifts up to the light, sheltering six science laboratories that share the flower-filled view in spring.

The vine-covered arcade gives the building a light, soft character facing the playground and the school campus to the east.

From within, the students' views onto nature encourages quiet contemplation

Photography by Gerrit Fokkema, Ben Guthrie

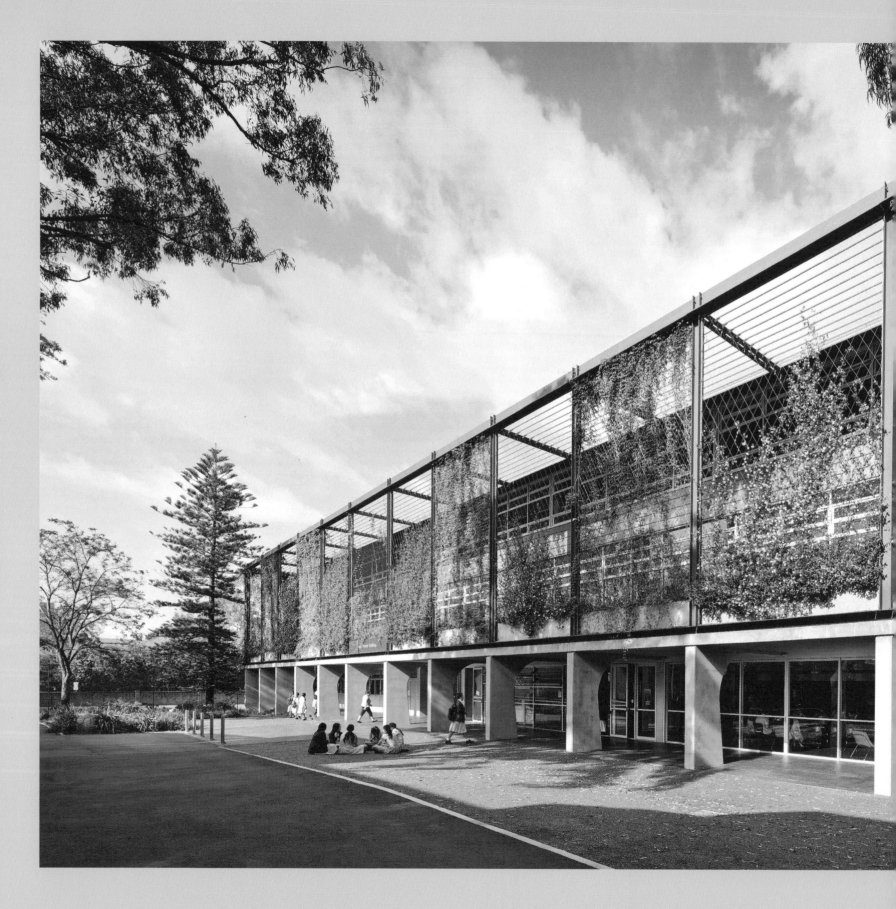

FLOATING IN A GREEN SEA

With design underway, **Centerbrook Architects** proposed the addition of a green roof to the project for aesthetic considerations. Before long, however, this extra feature would bear unexpected fruit. Ten centimetres (four inches) deep and blanketed with various sedums, the green roof forms part of an addition to the **Addison Gallery of American Art** at Phillips Academy Andover, a prestigious New England private school in Massachusetts, USA.

Views from inside to across the green roof are through a shroud of stainless steel mesh filter

The Addison is home to the only major art collection on an American high-school campus, and the new Learning Center would give patrons greater access to information and to the art itself, including works by Winslow Homer, Georgia O'Keeffe and Jackson Pollock.

The concept was that the roof's vegetation would soften the view out of the addition's glass curtain wall to the flat roof and the campus beyond. But even before construction began, civil engineers reported that the projected mitigation of rainwater run-off meant that a drainage system would not have to be upgraded as initially anticipated. This eliminated any concern that the green roof would put the project over budget.

The next happy development came when the museum was looking for a place to display recently donated glass sculptures by Dale Chihuly. All of the exhibition space was spoken for, so after gazing inward, the curators looked outside and determined that their new green roof was the perfect backdrop for Chihuly's installation of 10 spherical 'floats' (inspired by the glass floats used on fishing nets). The floats are not visible from the ground, but are in front of the wall of windows in the Addison's new museum learning centre. The glass floats are black with subtle hints of gold, purple, blue and green and they were soon floating in a sea of sedum, further enhancing the view from the centre.

The science faculty has since incorporated the roof into its curriculum: students track absorption rates, as well as the progress of invasive species. Finally, the town, which has experienced some recent flooding, loved this absorbent feature, the first within its borders. Officials now tout it as an example that other projects should consider.

Photography by Jeff Goldberg/Esto

The green roof of the new visitor centre in the **VanDusen Botanical Garden** in Vancouver, Canada, is designed to imitate the petals of an orchid and the central atrium of the building reflects the stamen, presenting an impressive and harmonious balance between architecture and nature.

The unusual orchid idea was conceived by the team at internationally renowned Canadian **Busby Perkins + Will Architects**, along with Canada's leading landscape architect, **Cornelia Hahn Oberlander** and **Sharp & Diamond Landscape Architecture Inc.**

Drawing inspiration from the organic shape of the orchid, the entire roof is designed as a number of undulating surfaces, representing the petals, which run off seamlessly into their surroundings at ground level. The pitch and curves of the roof areas range from 2° to 55° and were a considerable but not impossible challenge in terms of the actual wooden roof construction. A leakage-detection system was installed in the wooden roof,

followed by a double-layer, root-resistant bitumen waterproof membrane. **ZinCo** used three different system build-ups: the irrigation and protection layer BSM 64 was installed across the entire roof area. Then the System Build-up was installed with drainage and water storage element Floradrain® FD 40-E in those areas with a roof pitch of up to 10°. They installed Floraset® FS 75 elements in the areas with a roof pitch of up to 25° and Georaster® elements, which are specifically intended for steep-pitched roof areas of up to 55°.

The specific shape of the Floraset® elements provide sufficient interlocking with the substrate, and shear forces are diverted to the eaves upstand. With a steep-pitched roof, the 10-centimetre-high (4-inch-high) Georaster® elements that are connected to each other to create a stable and extensive unit and filled with substrate are used to secure the green roof. Additional shear barriers in this area will absorb any shear forces occurring.

The choice of plants and the prevailing microclimate (given the proximity to the coast) meant that permanent irrigation was not required. The green roof has more than 20 different types of plants and reflects the grass landscape native to this northeast Pacific region. In the flatter areas, for example, sedge (*Carex acuti-formis*) and rushes (*Juncus*) are used and in the pitched-roof areas yellow flag (*Iris pseudacorus*) and wild hyacinth (*Camassia*). These plants have all proven to be very efficient in breaking down ammonia, nitrate and phosphate. As a result, they contribute significantly to purifying rainwater or organic substances. For the steep-pitched roof areas, strongly drought-resistant sedum plants are used. With its biological diversity, the roof provides a habitat for a wide variety of bird and insect species.

Photography by ZinCo; Raymond Chan; Nic Lehoux; Courtesy: Perkins & Will

This design celebrates nature in an urban setting

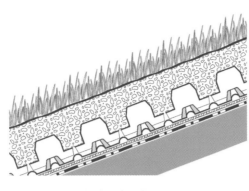

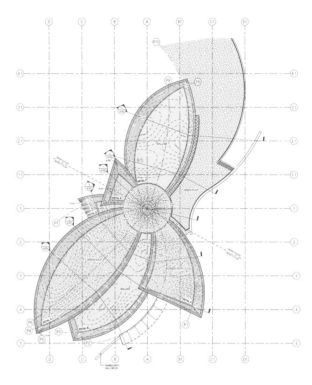

LETTING NATURE TAKE THE UPPER HAND

The **Paul Chevallier school complex** is situated in Rillieux-la-Pape, a northern suburb of Lyon, France. At 5,034 square metres (54,186 square feet) it's an unusually large project. The complex currently comprises a nursery school and an elementary school that are functionally and administratively autonomous. The schools are made up of rectangular modules in 'V' formations that enclose internal spaces – the nursery school includes a garden, and the elementary school has a patio.

One of the project's major characteristics is the relationship it establishes between architecture and nature: the structures are in keeping with their surroundings. The **Tectoniques Architects'** design takes into account the sloping terrain. The general profile is uniformly, deliberately low, harmonising with the slope in such a way that minimised excavation and foundation work.

The outer aspect of the complex is characterised by imposing green roof overhangs that are 2.4 metres long (7 feet, 8 inches) and 0.18 metres (0.59 feet) deep. Structurally, the roof is made of KLH® panels, while the upper storey has cavity floors in prefabricated laminates between OSB planking on dry slabs, with soft coverings.

The project harmonises the vegetation on the upper and lower levels: the broad, green roofs, with their waves of colour, separate the volumes in wood. The inclined roof planes and broad overhangs energise the silhouette, and attenuate the massiveness of the blocks.

Lending its tone to the entire project, this extra 'façade' represents the lyrical nature of the relationship between nature and architecture, in a Japanese-inspired atmosphere. The terrain is accessible and visible from inside the buildings via the first floor, part of which rises up over the roof and seems to float over this hanging garden.

From the inside, the large windows of the classrooms frame nature, and its close proximity makes it an element of the children's educational needs. The landscapers have provided children with places of discovery and experimentation, which include the walkways on the roofs, introducing the children to another ambiance. The nursery school is lower down on the slope. The ground plan is simple, so that the children can easily find their way around.

The collective spaces (library, concourse, music and computing rooms) stand out, in part, above the roofs. Large windows, sheltered by the roof projections and sunshades, open onto the playgrounds on the southern side, and the nursery school also receives natural light from the north.

Photography by Renaud Araud, Alain Vargas

The broad, pleated roofs unify the two schools

LIGHTING THE WAY

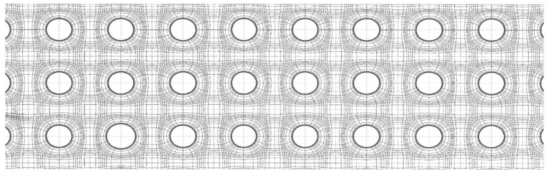

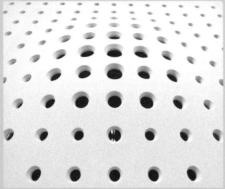

The new extension to Frankfurt's **Städel Museum** in Germany incorporates landscape, light, art and subtle architecture.

The project is the result of an international competition to design the extension of the museum, which would extend its exhibition space from 4,000 square metres (43,000 square feet) to 7,000 square metres (75,300 square feet). **schneider+schumacher's** winning design nearly doubled the exhibition area without compromising the openness of the museum – by burying the building beneath the museum's garden.

Beneath the gentle hill (which is landscaped upon the museum courtyard) there is a domed roof that looms over the new exhibition space. Twelve slim reinforced columns support the dome.

There are 195 circular skylights varying in diameter from 1.5 metres (4 feet, 11 inches) to 2.5 metres (8 feet, 2 inches) that punctuate the dome's concrete slab. These specially developed 'eyes for art' highlight the multi-disciplinary nature of the new extension – the apertures may both be walked upon as a collective art object, while illuminating the underground space with a rich sense of daylight that may be controlled by integrated LED lighting and built-in shading elements.

schneider+schumacher envisioned a central axis to extend the museum along its historic spatial sequence. The central foyer and all vertical access points were remodelled to allow wheelchair access. Below the water tables, 160 deep piles anchor the structure to prevent it from floating. The new building incorporates 36 geothermic piles that extend up to 82 metres (270 feet) into the earth to provide heat for cooler months and cooling for warmer months. The compact underground building form, the geothermic heating and cooling strategies and the large internal heat storage capacity together create an optimal room climate with minimal energy consumption.

Photography by Norbert Miguletz

The new extension is buried beneath the museum's garden

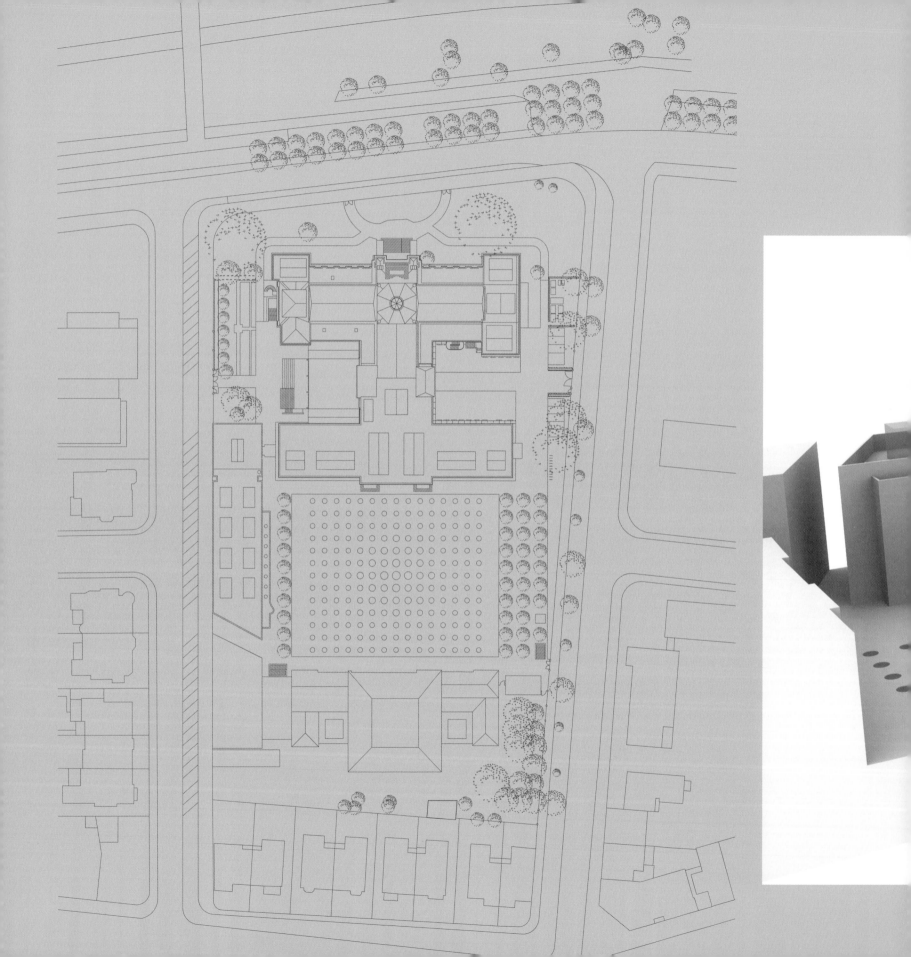

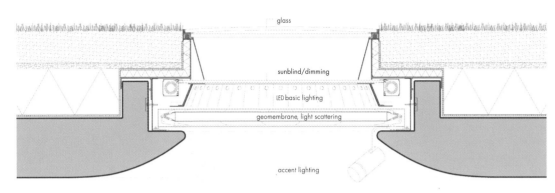

glass

sunblind/dimming

LED basic lighting

geomembrane, light scattering

accent lighting

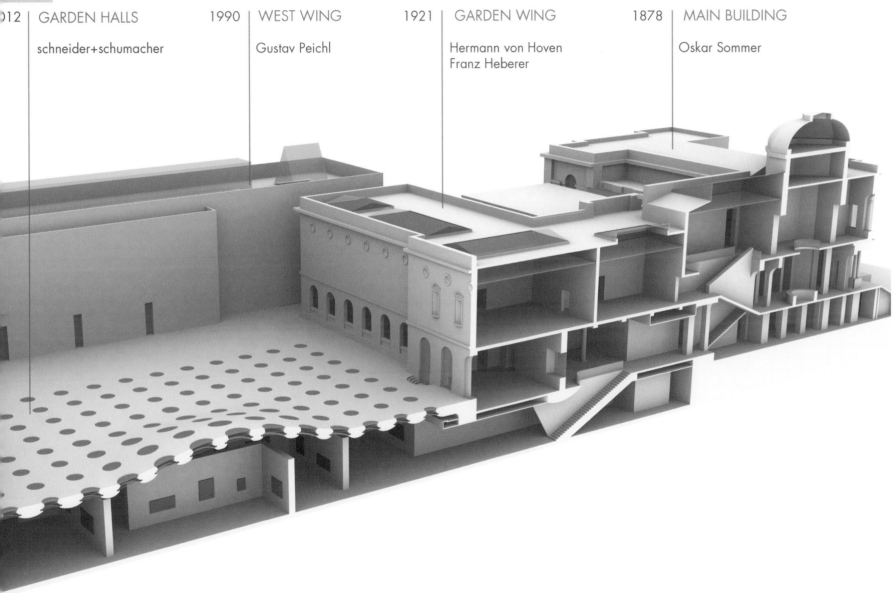

| 2012 | GARDEN HALLS | 1990 | WEST WING | 1921 | GARDEN WING | 1878 | MAIN BUILDING |

schneider+schumacher

Gustav Peichl

Hermann von Hoven
Franz Heberer

Oskar Sommer

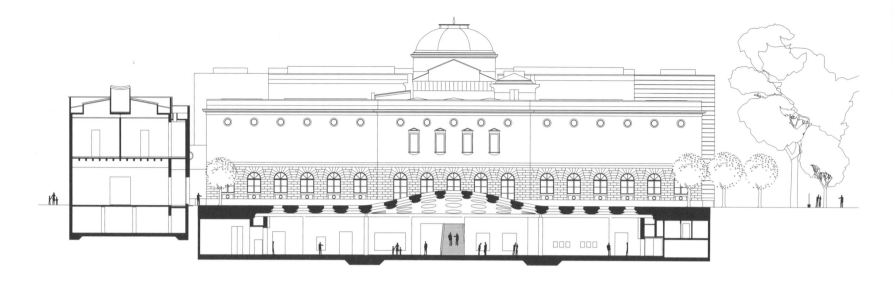

NURTURING THE
NEXT GENERATION

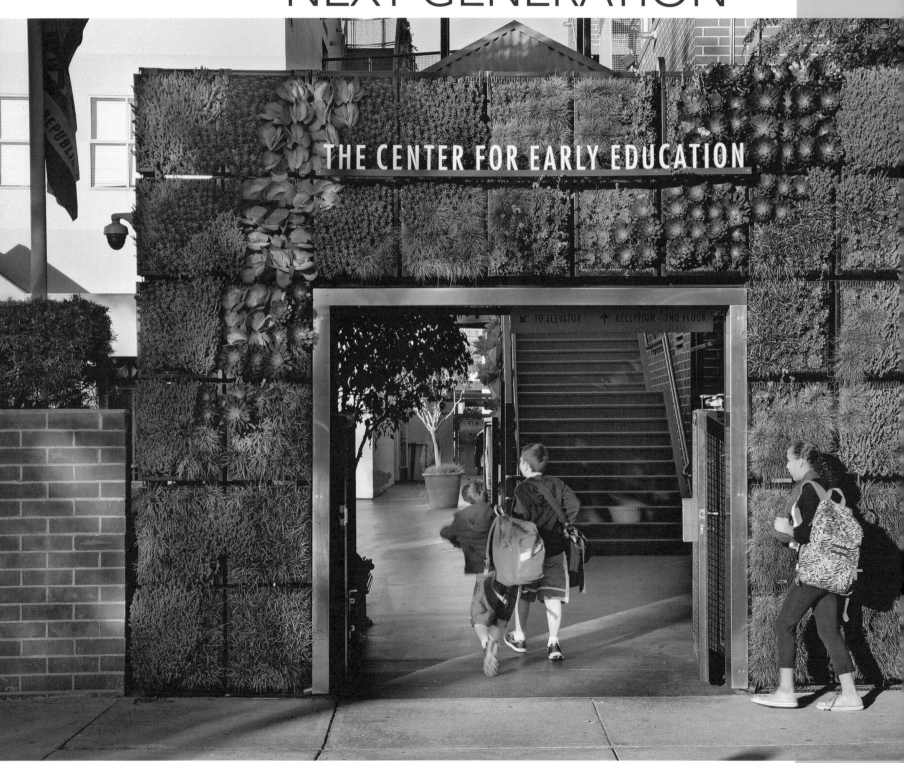

The **Center for Early Education** (CEE) is a socio-economically and culturally diverse independent school for children in Los Angeles, USA. The school embraces a philosophy of education that combines a nurturing, inclusive learning environment.

The CEE sought creative ways to boost the campus' sustainability and environmental education components. The school's greening process was underway with recycling, planting, and student awareness programs instituted in recent years. The task was challenging, given that pre-existing structures and the grounds could not be significantly altered. The program centered on a customised urban landscape and educational graphics program. Each element takes advantage of spatial opportunities to increase awareness about the environment, often by turning otherwise routine features of the building and its grounds into first-hand, experiential teaching and learning opportunities about environmental sustainability.

Rios Clementi Hale Studios and the CEE worked together to apply landscape programming to create an efficient, engaging and educational solution that brings a series of ecological learning moments to young children. The resulting features – or interventions – involve the school's main entryway, circulation paths, rooftop, and underground garage. The interventions include a distinctive, planted entranceway that forms a vertical landscape or living wall; pockets filled with native plants hanging from main outdoor circulation stairway railings; a rooftop turret containing a solar-powered weather station and an interactive wind turbine; and irrigation system that is fed from a collection tank in the underground garage to irrigate plants throughout the campus, while demonstrating water use and conservation.

A detailed graphic signage program boldly encourages students to 'water,' 'plant, seed & grow,' 'observe,' and 'collect.' The design connects the school to its local and regional environment by referencing plant ecologies from the surrounding areas, which are visible from the school's rooftops, as well as by celebrating the phenomenon of the bountiful watershed flowing underneath the school.

The experience begins with the vertical garden surrounding the school's main entrance – a 'green threshold' formed out of 34 vertical planter boxes containing a profusion of California succulents. A custom-made steel frame supports planter boxes. The backside of the planter boxes features exposed structure and irrigation pipes that are made visible to illustrate their function, along with storyboard graphics, maps and diagrams that are strategically sited in a heavily traversed spot, exposing the entire school community to CEE's environmental mission of water conservation, sustainable energy, cultivation of plants, and healthy living.

The building's pre-existing exterior circulation stairway was transformed into a living procession of regional plants growing within recycled plastic pouches. Plants native to the Santa Monica Mountains within the bright-blue felt-like containers made from recycled polypropylene are fed with exposed irrigation tubes and emitters.

The 'plant, seed & grow' functions are embodied in a rolling seed station showing the dynamics of planting, vegetation growth and composting. Students are able to tend seedlings and experience the growing and composting cycles in various locales on the campus; the mobile station can be rolled into sun and shade as needed.

Photography by Jim Simmons

The plants are selected from the natural ecology of the region

PLANNING A NARRATIVE

Spread across 17 hectares (42 acres) of lush green undulating land amid natural valleys, the **Taurian World School** at Ranchi in Jharkhand, India, has been designed by **Archohm** as a premier educational institute that promotes the holistic development of students. Based on a dream to create an ideal 'educational environment' and to redefine 'learning' in terms of facility and ambience, the school uses an innovative spatial palette with high-level technology and superior-quality materials.

Entry is via a majestic, white, perforated metal gate, which is automated and centrally rotated to bi-furcate traffic towards a sleek state-of-the-art sports and culture facility block. The sports block's rooftop cantilevered basketball court serves as a viewing deck to the entire campus, especially the sporting facilities and the semi Olympic swimming pool just beyond. It also demonstrates the value and importance of open spaces, by transferring a usual ground function to a higher level without losing its characteristics; it both increases visibility and adds a dynamic hierarchy to the open spaces.

Beyond this a steel bridge spans over a cluster of play areas, leading to the main administration block. The two side façades of this block have been kept completely blank so as to direct attention to the central glass core. From the bridge, one can also get glimpses of the library's reading bays.

The administration block then dramatically opens up into a large courtyard bound by class rooms on the opposite side, a pleasant route that carries students into the secure environment of shades, greens and courtyards.

The class-room blocks are designed as staggered modules and are positioned to contain a variety of small spaces that can combine to form a large central assembly space. The façades of these blocks facing the court have a large glass panel that reflects the semi-open spaces at the upper level. This allows common spaces to be used for a variety of activities and also lets the façades act as effective sound barriers.

The hostel blocks have been designed in horseshoe forms with grass rooftops and individual courtyards. The slanting roofs help prevent heat absorption and promote rainwater harvesting.

Being away from the pollution of the city and in the midst of valleys, the school has a zero pollution ambience with a natural environment that is reflected throughout the campus. One of the key aspects of the design process was to create a school that would preserve the greenness and openness of the existing site.

Hierarchies of open/semi-open spaces are used as innovative interaction hubs that also act as sound barriers and effective linking spaces. The inclusion of 'nature' is also an attempt to make students realise the vastness of the world and help liberate their young minds.

Photography by Joy Datta

Emphasis has been given to provide spaces between buildings rather than within them

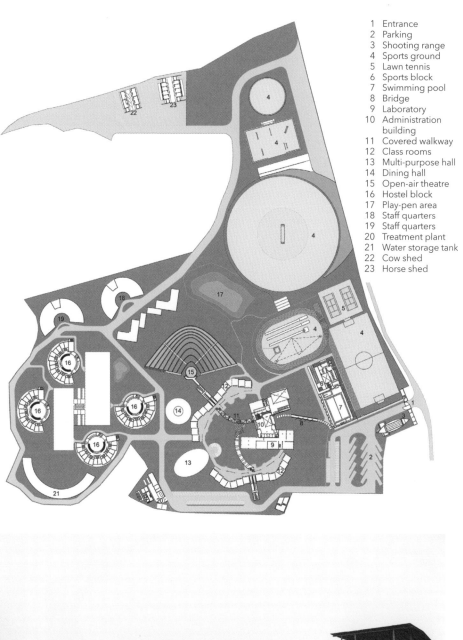

1 Entrance
2 Parking
3 Shooting range
4 Sports ground
5 Lawn tennis
6 Sports block
7 Swimming pool
8 Bridge
9 Laboratory
10 Administration
   building
11 Covered walkway
12 Class rooms
13 Multi-purpose hall
14 Dining hall
15 Open-air theatre
16 Hostel block
17 Play-pen area
18 Staff quarters
19 Staff quarters
20 Treatment plant
21 Water storage tank
22 Cow shed
23 Horse shed

READING BY THE LANTERN

The **Mediatheque Mont de Marsan** (Media Library) is a strong cultural symbol for the Marsan urban area. It is a place of discovery, gatherings and exchanges for its users. It is a visible, distinctive building.

The Media Library stands in the middle of the Bosquet barracks at Mont de Marsan, France, and the architectural firm, **archi5**, has taken care to augment the dialogue with the location's strong architectural whole. With its clean envelope of pure geometric lines, at 60 square metres (197 square feet), the building complies with the classical layout yet contrasts with its austerity by offsetting the system with a corner opening onto the city. Its façades reflect the surrounding barracks like a respectful, deferential mirror.

The building has been designed as a covered cultural square by making the façades transparent and the floor uniform, also through its position in the middle of the barracks. This design is read by extending the planted roof to make it seem to be hovering above the ground.

The grassy incline that surrounds the building draws the eye upwards, then gives way to alternating transparent and reflecting glass façades. The green roof serves to root the building into its grassy, hilly surroundings.

The Media Library's central location in the military drill yard inspired a building with four main sides, varying from one another by simply adapting to the direction they face. The Media Library confirms its identity from whatever angle it is viewed; at night it becomes a lantern that brings the square to life, turning it into an inviting, open and transparent space.

The interior space on the ground floor is completely open and revolves around a patio, the design of which has been inspired by Matisse's paintings of acanthus leaves, and the volumes of which recall Alvar Aalto's vases. It may well be this 'surprise' – almost hidden – patio that makes the building so popular with the public.

Photography by Sergio Grazia, Marsan Agglomération

The extension of a planted roof makes the building appear to hover above the ground

INDUSTRIAL INTELLIGENCE

COMBINING SOLAR ENERGY & GREEN ROOFING

Schiphol Airport Amsterdam has had an extensive green roof since the 1980s, but the roof's pre-existing insulating package – a waterproof membrane and green roof based on rock wool panels – could no longer function in the long term. The material 'rock wool' lost a lot of substance over the years and as a result the plants were failing.

The work has been done in collaboration with **BOKO** and **Wieringen Prins Hoveniers**. The photovoltaic system that's been integrated into the green roof hence makes it the first building in the Netherlands to combine green roofing with a solar energy system on such a large scale.

The roof is approximately 8,600 square metres (28,215 square feet) in size; it has limited load capacity reserves and a roof pitch of between 4° and 10°. It is slightly vaulted and slopes down towards the ground on all sides. Triangular skylights with a counter slope interrupt the roof area and are also greened.

Once the old roof build-up was removed, a solid base was created using a root-resistant, bituminous roof waterproof membrane. For the required combination of green and solar, **ZinCo** used the

suitable system build-up 'SolarVert' with Fixodrain® XD 20. This system build-up is specially designed for large-scale roofs. It is based on the drainage and water retention sheet Fixodrain® XD 20, which has a pre-laminated filter sheet on the upper side and is supplied in rolls. In order to address the issue of roof pitch, a rubber protection layer was laminated onto the underside of the Fixodrain® XD 20 sheet as an anti-slip device.

Once the solar bases were in place the substrate layer was added. The pre-calculated ballast provided by the roof substrate secures the mounting frames for the solar modules and holds them in place, even during a storm. The substrate was levelled to create a good basis for the 'Sedum Carpet' plant mats, thus providing instant greenery.

The green roof provides not only the ballast required to anchor the solar system but also improves the efficiency of the unit, because a green roof provides for a lower ambient temperature than a bare or gravelled roof. Other benefits of a green roof are rainwater retention, noise prevention, improvement of the microclimate and the provision of a habitat for fauna and flora.

Photography by ZinCo, Wieringen Prins Hoveniers

The green roof will protect the roof membrane from temperature fluctuation and, therefore, from premature ageing

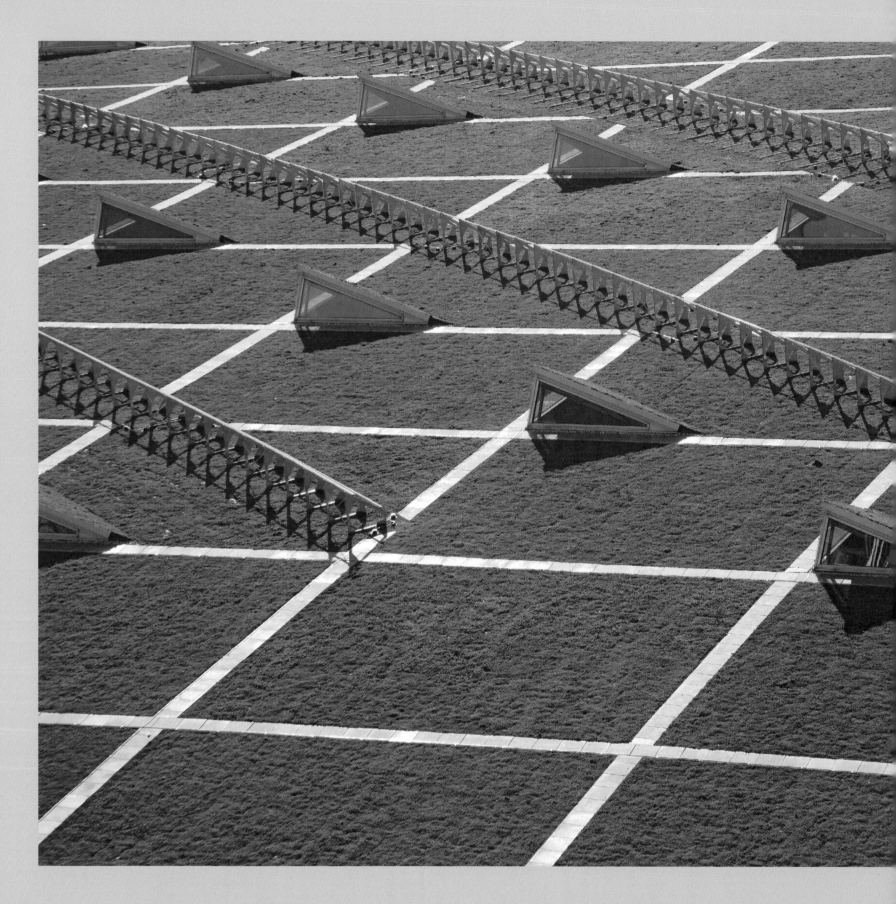

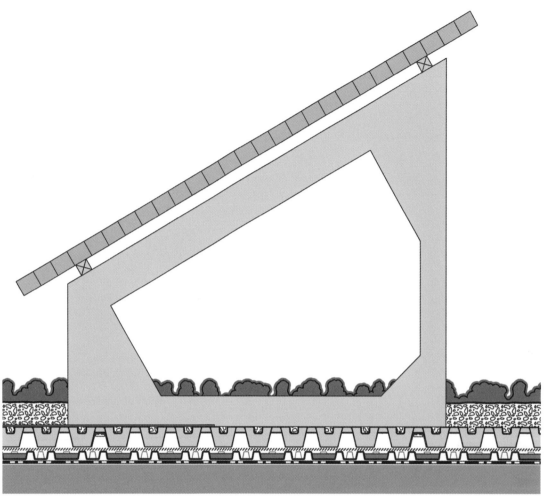

The **Victorian Desalination Project** in Wonthaggi, Victoria, Australia, brings together architecture, ecology, landscape and world-class technology to create one of the most significant environmental design projects featuring an innovative green roof, and which integrates the plant's buildings with the landscape.

The design team's conceptual approach, led by **ASPECT Studios** with **ARM** and **PVH** architects, drew on antecedents including the history of land art, and the history of the site itself, to create an overarching design palimpsest. An important component of this conceptual diagram was the green roof systems applied to key buildings within the plant, as part of the strong gesture of integration between the site and the plant.

This process involved a comprehensive review of green roof design standards and technologies worldwide, and adaptation of these to the unique environmental and climatic factors of the site. Consideration was given to four key aspects of green roof design, namely: weight; water; wind; and plants in developing a design and maintenance strategy.

The green roof design, which covers 26,000 square metres (279,861 square feet), has overcome a number of barriers, and developed a series of enabling technologies, including a light weight substrate with high water-holding capability and air-filled porosity; a measure to mitigate the effects of the high winds; an irrigation strategy that mitigates the regular extreme heat events; inclusion of a leak detection system; and a technique for selection of plants that assess the locally occurring plant species for the traits that lend them to be successful colonisers of the green roof.

Photography by Thiess Degrémont Joint Venture, ASPECT Studios, Fytogreen Australia

The green roof planting includes pigface, a succulent-like, spreading groundcover with large flowers

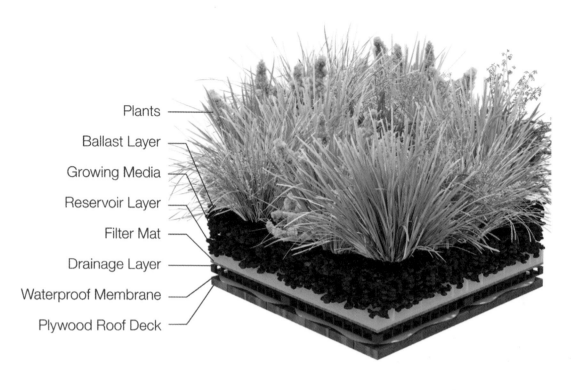

Plants
Ballast Layer
Growing Media
Reservoir Layer
Filter Mat
Drainage Layer
Waterproof Membrane
Plywood Roof Deck

MAKING WAVES

Located in Sotteville lès Rouen, France, **Marcel Sembat High School** offers technical education in bodyworks and auto mechanics. The project involved refurbishment of the existing school buildings, including new workshops, which need substantial height and volume. The new workshops also need to respond to the school's social setting: suburban environment, technical training and cars.

The building design, headed by the **archi5** studio, sought to restore unity to the school and give it a visual identity of strength and modernity. This was achieved by reconnecting it with its surroundings, particularly with the workshop building, so that its soft lines and slopes blended naturally and harmoniously into the physical features of the neighbouring park.

The flagship of this project – namely, the building that houses the workshops – comprises sheets of steel that, just like waves, gently lap the adjoining park and flow over existing structures.

The building extends from the park's boundary and gently blends into the site thanks to the undulating feature of its rolling vegetated roof gardens, which undulate across the buildings' steel-blade frameworks. The supporting steel structures hold 8,000 square metres (26,247 square feet) of green roof and contribute to the building's thermal inertia, protecting the inside environment against drastic changes in temperature, and provide effective sound insulation and waterproofing. The green roofing

All the industrial technology classrooms and workshops have now been gathered under the same roof

is designed to swoop to the ground, creating internal courtyards that act as skylights to the surrounding spaces.

This also helped to achieve one the project's main objectives: to bring more light into the buildings, as well as change the views overlooking public areas. For this purpose translucent polycarbonate and glass was used for the façade, and little patios were built to form pools of light between the sheets of steel. The two sites,

cut across by a road, are joined by the creation of a new public area that connects the school with the new library.

Steel is used as the tool of formal creation and here it takes a prominent role in the project's design. Steel has quickly become the perfect solution: guaranteeing connection, undulation, free volumes and the appearance of strength.

Photography by Sergio Grazia, Thomas Jorion

MEDIATING BETWEEN FOREST & GRASSLAND

This undulating roof serves as an arresting crown for the **Hotchkiss School biomass heating plant**, proclaiming the project's pre-eminent greenness and contributing to its LEED certification. The design by **Centerbrook Architects** accomplishes divergent goals: it makes infrastructure alluring by creating an iconic presence on this independent school campus; while the low-slung structure, whose vegetated roof is the colour of surrounding flora, melds with its bucolic environs.

The 1600-square-metre (16,500-square-foot) plant in Connecticut, USA, provides heat for 600 students and faculty and 85 buildings, but there were other project objectives: reduce greenhouse gas emissions to help the school become carbon neutral by 2020; lower utility costs with a local sustainable fuel, in place of foreign oil; and do double-duty as a classroom by exposing green systems and materials to close observation and study.

Sustainably harvested woodchips, an IPCC-designated renewable fuel, replace 567,812 litres (150,000 gallons) of imported fuel oil annually, cutting emissions, most dramatically sulfur dioxide, by 90 percent. Waste ash is collected for use as fertiliser on student-tended gardens. During the first winter, the school reported substantial savings in heating costs.

Supporting the roof are glue-laminated timber trusses, a manufactured wood product that optimises the structural values of this renewable resource. Glulam has less embodied energy than reinforced concrete or steel and can be used for longer spans, heavier loads, and complex shapes. Other local and renewable wood products were used throughout for framing, railings, veneer, and composite wallboards.

To make the building an ancillary classroom a specially designed mezzanine affords views of plant operations and also houses an exhibit on the biomass process and sustainable construction. The vegetated green roof is part of the curriculum. An outdoor pathway lets students observe how rainwater not absorbed by the sedum is filtered, then channeled through newly created rain gardens and bio-swales to replenish nearby wetlands. A mixture of sedums has been selected to thrive in the microclimate of the roof as well as New England's seasonal fluctuations. Its layers of soil and plants provide insulation and extend the life of the structure below.

The green roof visually blends in with the natural landscape

Photography by David Sundberg/Esto

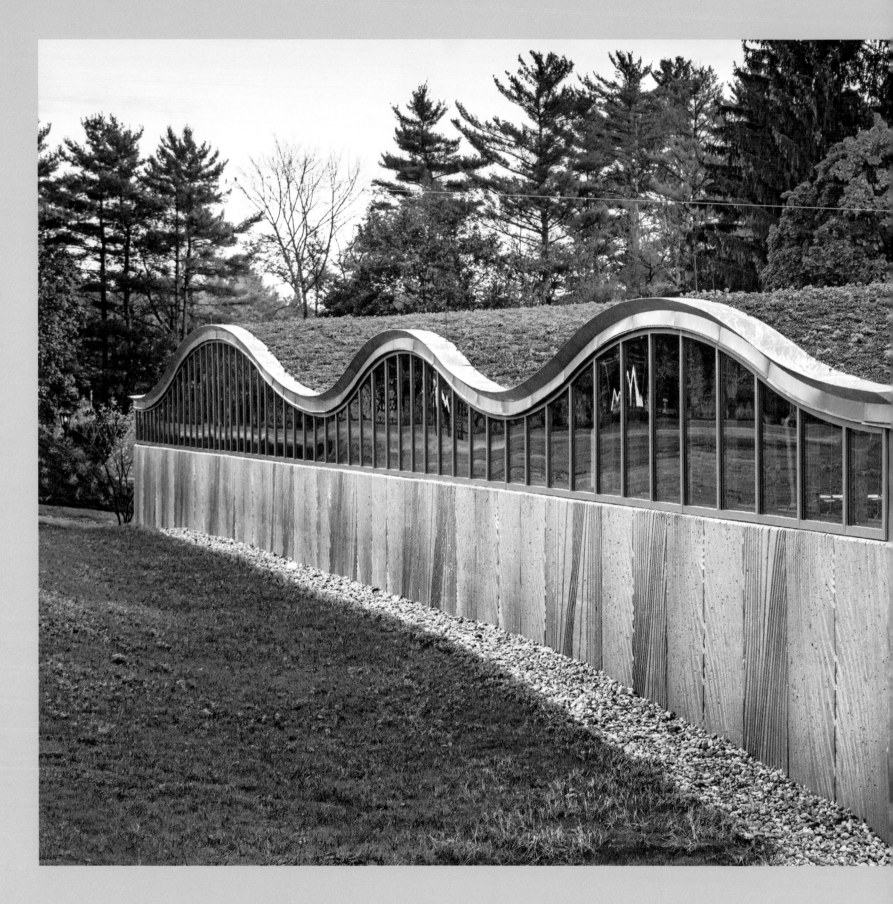

Landscape architect **James Corner Field Operations** worked in collaboration with **ZinCo** and the renowned plant designer **Piet Oudolf** to create an attractive 'green belt' of New York's former elevated railway line. The line was built on stilts between blocks of houses and sits at a height of 5 to 9 metres (16 feet, 4 inches to 29 feet, 6 inches) and a width of between 9 and 18 metres (29 feet, 6 inches and 59 feet).

The concept for the **High Line Park** included ponds and benches, as with other parks. The park is as wide as the tracks once were: so wide that two freight trains could pass by at a time. The Hudson River, the Empire State Building and the Statue of Liberty are visible from various viewing points and access to the park is at regular intervals by means of staircases or lifts. The planners aimed to retain the character of the natural flora and wilderness that had been allowed to flourish there, undisturbed, for 20 years. The tracks remain visible, to remind people of their provenance.

The walkways consist of a concrete 'planking' system where the planks taper to one end, which allow the boundaries between hard and soft surfaces to become blurred. This homogenous walkway, with its intensive green roofing, is a connecting element along the entire length of the High Line, guiding the park visitors at times along a narrow path and at other times along a wider stretch through greenery.

Where the High Line becomes narrower, there is a path at a height of 2.5 metres (8 feet, 2 inches) over the level of the former tracks, so that visitors can saunter along as if on a catwalk – beneath the leafy overhang created by the high trees.

ZinCo-Floradrain® elements are the chosen drainage system for the green roofing, and this system is installed across the entire surface, even beneath the existing supply lines for water and electricity. These moulded drainage elements have storage cells on their upper side for storing precipitation. Excess water, on the other hand, is safely drained away through the channel system below.

There are 210 plant species, including many shrubs and trees that are thriving on a substrate with an average depth of about 45 centimetres (17 inches). The design of the park allows for a great mix of microclimates, from very wet, moor-like zones to vegetation with dry, steppe grass. Ornamental growth is not wanted here, over-growing is purposely included in the plan.

The benches 'growing out of the ground' encourage visitors to pause for a moment during their stroll, and a multi-level seating area resembling a theatre enables people to watch the traffic on the street below through a glass pane.

Photography by ZinCo

The 'longest green roof in the world'

RESIDENTIAL STYLE

BLENDING INTO THE HILLSIDE

The clients for the **Mill Valley Cabins** in California, USA, wished to add some accessory structures to their existing hillside home. Programmatically, the clients sought to provide space for an artist studio and a separate yoga space that would also serve as a private guest cabin. **Feldman Architecture** divided the program into two small cabins and placed them lightly between existing trees in order to minimise the re-grading of the steep hillside.

The upper level is devoted to the art studio, which offers privacy for the artist working within and which overlooks the lower-level yoga studio. The orientation of the two cabins captures different views. The yoga studio is minimally furnished with beautiful views of the tree canopy, and its roof has been planted with a garden since the upper building would be looking down onto it.

The focus of the yoga studio's roof design was to make the building blend into the natural forest surroundings, enabling the views from the art studio to extend over the lush hillside. The roof garden includes a variety of sedum plantings that are arranged in a banded pattern. The plants retain a lot of moisture and require minimal maintenance.

Photography by Joe Fletcher

The green roofs provide additional space for the clients' love of gardening

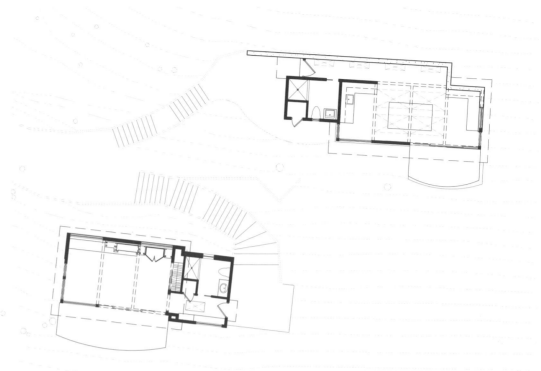

CARVING OUT A HOUSE

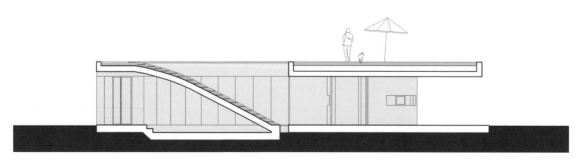

A green clearing surrounded by forest, on the outskirts of Warsaw, Poland, was the only context for the proposed small **OUTrial House**. Hence the idea to 'carve out' a piece of the grass-covered site, move it up and treat it as the roofing to arrange all the required functions underneath.

When the whole was ready, the client came up with another request for **KWK Promes**: to create some space for a small recording studio and a conservatory. The latter was obtained by linking the ground floor with the grassy roof through an 'incision' in the green plane and 'bending' the incised fragment down, inside the building.

This procedure turned the roof into an atrium, as the only way to reach it was through the interior of the house. As opposed, however, to a typical atrium, the newly created space has all the advantages of an outer garden while remaining a safe, internal zone within the building.

This way, a new type of house was created, and its designation – OUTrial – is to convey the idea of an atypical atrium, forming part of both the interior and the exterior of the building.

The studio was created in a similar way as the conservatory, but in order to ensure work comfort for a rock musician, it was isolated from the rest of the house by shifting it upwards.

Photography by Juliusz Sokotowski

OUTrial conveys the idea of an atypical atrium, forming part of both the interior and the exterior of the building

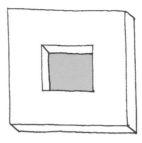

Atrial house

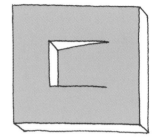

OUTrial house

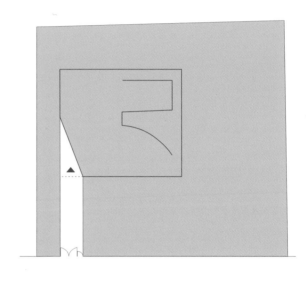

Situation

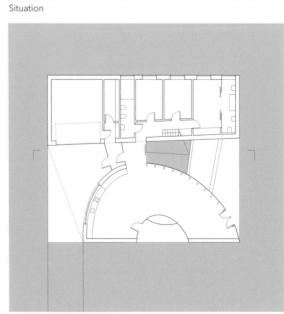

Ground floor plan

FENCING IN THE WALLS

This vertical Fytogreen **garden wall** system has been designed as an extension to a dividing blade wall between two side-by-side townhouses located in Melbourne, Australia. The firm **Saaj Design** has built this garden to form the 'fence' between the townhouses, and created a space for external wall art from the internal view.

The wall panel is comparatively large relative to the scale of the house, measuring 4.5 metres (14 feet, 9 inches) wide by 3 metres (9 feet, 10 inches) tall. It faces north and is framed by black powder-coated panels and a silver mirror. The mirror adds to the illusions of the 'floating garden'.

The choice of drought-hardy plant types explores succulent textures and dramatic colour. The wall comprises the stunning, shallow-rooted Echeveria 'Black Prince' with mounds of Sedum moss in striking gold as background coverage. The plants move from east to west and graduate from chartreuse green to dark chocolate to black/red, and in unison the garden wall graduates visually from the townhouse interior to the exterior's traditional garden. The wall panels feature a concealed watering system that requires approximately one bucket per session, offering an efficient, drought-tolerant option.

Photography by Andrew Bartholomeusz

This green wall acts as a fence between two townhouses

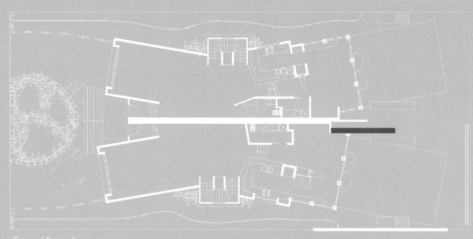
Ground-floor plan

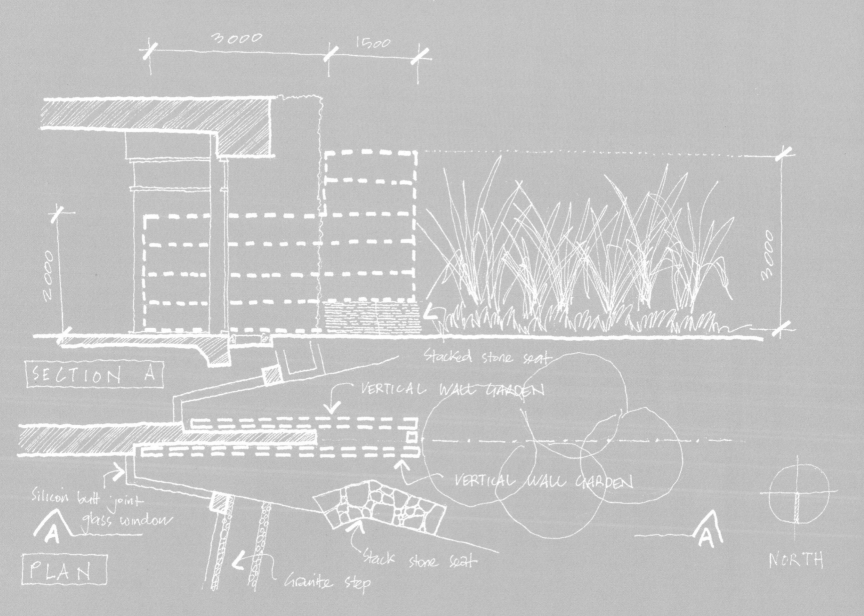

3000   1500

2000

3000

SECTION A

Stacked stone seat

VERTICAL WALL GARDEN

VERTICAL WALL GARDEN

Silicon butt joint
glass window

PLAN

Stack stone seat

Granite step

NORTH

GARDENING IN THE SKY

Roof Plan   1 Sedum plantings

Green roofs on each level effectively reduces the footprint of the house to zero

Approximately half the size of a typical new house in Toronto, Ontario, Canada, and designed by **LGA Architectural Partners** for long-term use with plenty of environmental and flexibility features, the **Euclid Avenue House** design presents a viable new sustainable housing prototype.

All the roofs levels have been planted with a range of drought-resistant plant types and edible plants in lieu of the traditional grass lawn requiring inordinate amounts of water and pesticides. The rooftop garden, also accessible through the master bedroom, is planted with hostas (also known as plantain lilies), native grasses and fragrant lavender

that are indigenous to Ontario. These plantings impact the owners' experience of their property, prompting them to learn about how planting attracts birds or butterflies, and how the water run-off affects the plants in the garden below.

The live roofs help to keep the building interiors cool in the summer; they reduce the amount of heat reflected into the atmosphere and heat build-up, which reduces the ambient air temperature, cuts down on light pollution and improves the local air quality through the filtering of carbon emissions so common in developed environments.

In addition to the insulation provided by the green roofs, the house is kept reasonably cool by a design that maximises the cross breezes that consistently blow through east/west operable windows and by ceiling fans. An 'on-demand' gas-fired hot-water boiler heats both the water for the radiant floors and the domestic hot water. All of the storm water collected by the house is reused on site. The hard landscaping materials are all local and all exterior lighting is solar generated.

Photography by Ben Rahn / A-Frame Inc.

INTEGRATING OBJECT & ENVIRONMENT

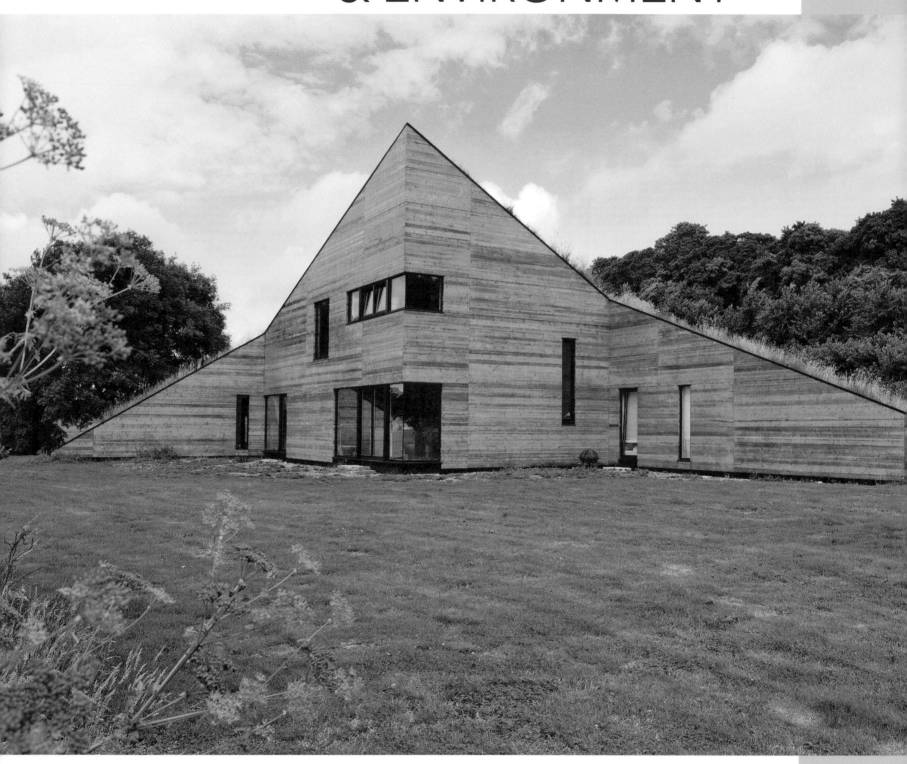

The work of **Mark Merer** investigates the union of object and environment, its physical relationship with the ground and how it translates into a building.

The initial idea to develop an environmentally sensitive scheme for an allocated development area started with the studying of placement and the watching of objects in clay and sand creating shapes through the interaction of the wind and rain.

One aspect of the work developed into the basic forms using triangulation, and this work was the basis of a collaborative project completed in the USA, between Mark Merer, the Swinomish tribal people of Fidalgo Island in Washington State, USA, and another architectural firm, Landhouse. This resulted in a housing project that was a sensitive to the beliefs and traditions of the Swinomish and which bore some resemblance to their surroundings.

The structure of **Welham Studios**, built in Somerset, UK, is based on housing module units developed as a concept for the Swinomish project, which incorporated module units comprising elder, student, single family, vacation, multifamily and community facilities. A variety of layouts had been designed, including three basic sizes. Welham Studios is the largest of the three designs. The studios are where Mark Merer and his wife, artist Lucy Glendinning, work.

The building is constructed using a curved grass roof rising up from the ground over a glulam timber framework. The frame is covered in structurally insulated panels of thermoform three-ply cladding that came in 5-metre by 2-metre (16 feet, 4 inches by 6 feet, 5 inches) sheets. The roofing material is an EPDM membrane with an inbuilt root barrier, a 100mm substrate with wildflower meadow turf.

Photography by Louis Porter

Mark states: *"You become very much more aware of the landscape by putting objects in it."*

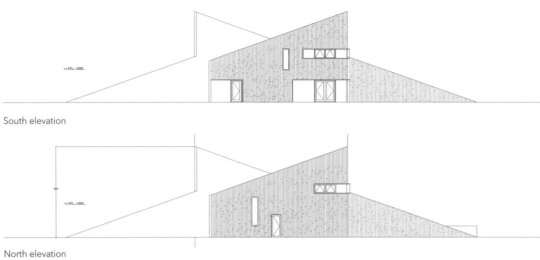

South elevation

North elevation

The four-storey **Sky Garden House** is designed with a central void and largely shallow volumes, particularly on the upper floors, which maximize cross ventilation and reduce dependence on mechanical air conditioning.

The large, shaded areas of glazing on most rooms reduce the reliance on artificial lighting during daylight hours while minimising solar gain, and the large acrylic window in the basement-level media room floods it with diffused natural light, further reducing energy consumption. The gardens on each level typically overhang the storey below, providing shade and reducing overheating in Singapore's tropical climate.

Guz Architects' concept of Sky Garden House is strongly influenced by the ambition of enhancing the occupant's quality of life. This is largely achieved by the roof gardens on every level. As well as having direct access to these, interior spaces have large areas of glazing with views out over the gardens to the sea and sky. The large amount of natural daylight brought in contributes strongly to a good indoor environment. Large acrylic windows in the pool result in even the basement receiving great amounts of diffused natural light.

The design of the open-air stairwell cutting through the centre of the building reduces the depth of indoor areas and encourages cross ventilation. Using the natural cross ventilation to its potential, along with the assistance of mechanical ventilation when necessary, produces a high indoor air quality.

The integration of 'Sky Garden House' with nature and the outdoors is most evident in the garden areas on every level. The gardens, with much planting and a number of trees, reduce carbon dioxide and help counter greenhouse gas emissions. The large areas of grass absorb much less heat than conventional roofing materials resulting in less thermal storage in the building itself, reducing the use of cooling systems.

In Singapore's tropical climate, with its heavy rains, water retention of garden areas also contributes to reducing the pressure on the surface water system at peak times.

The roof curves gently like a small hill

Photography courtesy of Guz Architects

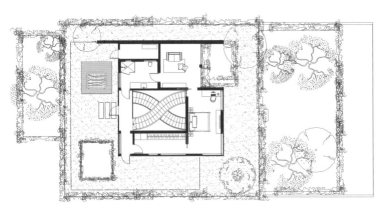

Third floor 1:200

Second floor 1:200

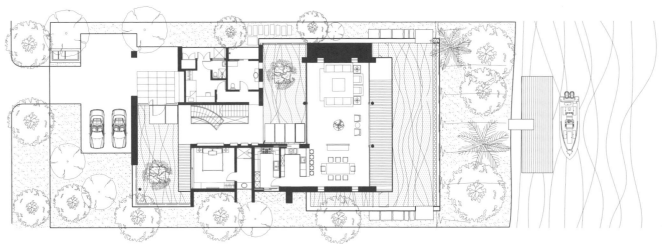

First floor 1:200

LIVING IN A VERTICAL SUBURBIA

The Mountain is located in Orestad city and offers the best of two worlds: closeness to the hectic city life in the centre of Copenhagen, Denmark, and the tranquillity characteristic of suburban life. The Mountain appears as a suburban neighbourhood of garden homes flowing over a 10-storey building – suburban living with urban density.

The program, designed by **BIG CHP**, was for two-thirds parking and one-third living. Rather than doing two separate buildings next to each other – a parking section and a housing block – it was decided to merge the two functions into a symbiotic relationship. The parking area needs to be connected to the street, and the homes require sunlight, fresh air and views, thus all apartments have roof gardens facing the sun, amazing views and parking on the 10th floor. The parking area has become the base upon which to place terraced housing, like a concrete hillside covered by a thin layer of housing, cascading from the top floor to the street edge.

The residents of the 80 apartments will be the first in Orestad to have the possibility of parking directly outside their homes. The gigantic parking area contains 480 parking spots and a sloping elevator that moves along the mountain's inner walls. In some places the ceiling height is up to 16 metres (52 feet), which gives the impression of a cathedral-like space.

The roof gardens consist of a terrace and a garden with plants changing character according to the seasons. The building has a huge watering system that maintains the roof gardens. The only thing that separates the apartment and the garden is a glass façade with sliding doors to provide light and fresh air.

The north and west façades are covered by perforated aluminium plates, which let in air and light to the parking area. The holes in the façade form a huge reproduction of Mount Everest. During the day the holes in the aluminium plates will appear black on the bright aluminium, and the gigantic picture will resemble that of a rough rasterized photo. At night time the façade will be lit from the inside and appear as a photo negative in different colours as each floor in the parking area has different colours.

Photography by Jakob Boserup, Ulrik Jantzen, Jens Lindhe, Dragor Luftfoto, Carsten Kring, Matteo Sartori, Traeprisen

Combining the splendours of the suburban backyard with the social intensity of urban density

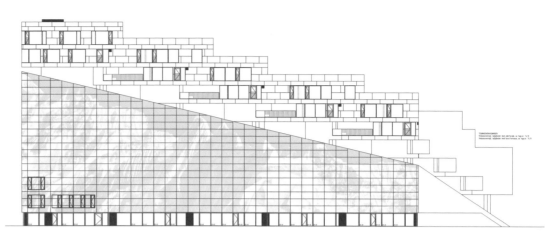

Located on a rehabilitated brownfield site, **Edgeland House** is a modern re-interpretation of one of the oldest housing typologies in North America, the Native American pit house. The pit house, typically sunken, takes advantage of the earth's mass to maintain thermal comfort throughout the year. Edgeland's relationship to the landscape, both in terms of approach as well as building performance involves an insulative green roof and a 2.13-metre (7-foot) excavation – gaining benefits from the earth's mass to help it stay cooler in the summer and warmer in the winter.

Such an architectural setting presents an opportunity for maximum energy efficiency when combined with high-performance systems, such as the integrated hydronic HVAC system. The mechanical system combines hydronic heating and cooling, geothermal heat exchange, phase-change thermal heat storage and a green roof for maximum energy efficiency.

This **Bercy Chen Studio** project, located in Texas, USA, is about healing the land and ameliorating the scars of the site's industrial past. The project raises awareness about a diminishing natural landscape and its finite resources by creating a balance between the surrounding industrial zone and the natural river residing on opposite side of the site. Formerly a brownfield area occupied by an oil pipeline, measures were taken to ensure the safety of surrounding people and vegetation as the pipe was excavated.

Edgeland's relationship to the landscape and the green mechanical system that sustains it are two of the most innovative aspects of the project. Buried below the earth's surface with an insulative green roof, Edgeland House makes use of the earth's thermal mass to maintain thermal comfort throughout the year. This gesture also aids in maximising the efficiency of the hydronic heating and cooling system that is tied to: geothermal wells, and slab and ceiling loops. The efficiency of the hydronic system is further bolstered by the use of phase-change materials built into the water tanks, which serve to neutralise loads on the heat pump.

The project also features a smart pool that provides an additional thermal mass that ties into the geothermal system. Additionally, the smart pool features a high-tech, chlorine-free water purification system that uses a diamond electrode plate to disinfect. Local products were used where possible and materials were chosen for performance and durability, reducing maintenance costs in the long run.

Photography by Paul Bardagjy

Edgeland House makes use of the earth's thermal mass to maintain thermal comfort throughout the year

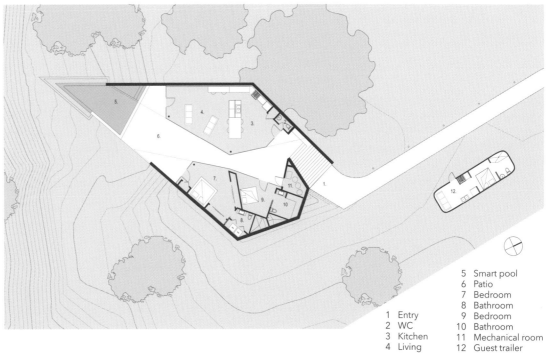

5 Smart pool
6 Patio
7 Bedroom
8 Bathroom
9 Bedroom
10 Bathroom
11 Mechanical room
12 Guest trailer

1 Entry
2 WC
3 Kitchen
4 Living

The **2 Bar** home in Menlo Park, California, USA, represents a cost-conscious design and implementation of green materials and technologies for a couple with two young children. The new residence is a smart, sustainable, open home that embraces the family's indoor/outdoor lifestyle. The 2 Bar concept, by **Feldman Architecture**, floats a bedroom bar above and perpendicular to a living bar, an arrangement that allows both spaces to open up to more light than the typical box. The lower, living level features accordion and lift/slide doors that allow the house to open to a generous backyard and garden.

A private, green roof with a deck allows the upper level to also have a connection to garden and landscape. The roof is planted with sedum plants and river rock edging, and the overhang helps to control solar heat gain while still allowing in plenty of natural light. The horizontal slats that clad the upper bar create a simple and elegant rain screen and provide operable panels over the windows that can be easily moved to control light, heat and privacy.

The residence has a compact and efficient layout that also meets the client's concerns regarding costs and environmental consciousness for sustainable materials and systems: renewable bamboo is used for the flooring and cabinets, and the kitchen features clerestory windows to allow in natural light, along with a photovoltaic array.

Photography by Joe Fletcher

A private deck on the green roof offers a quiet outdoor space off the master bedroom

GARAGE
18' x 19'

SITTING
11' x 17'

KITCHEN
8' x 13'

LIVING
15' x 20'

M. BA

BR 1
11' x 10'

M. BR
12' x 10'

BR 2
11' x 10'

NESTLING INTO THE HILLSIDE

The hilltop residence of **Leicester House**, located at the edge of a wooded knoll in the rolling foothills of the Blue Ridge Mountains in North Carolina, USA, has expansive southern and western views. Approaching the house through these woods, one arrives at a striking single-storey façade of corten steel in a wood frame, designed by **SPG Architects**. A hint of the views is provided through the glass door, but it is not until entry that the full impact of the hilltop views is experienced. The rear glass walls, which face west and south, are shielded by large overhangs and open to rolling farmland below and the mountains beyond.

The entry level serves as the primary living area comprised of living, dining, kitchen, study and master bedroom suite. A two-bedroom guest wing with a media room is carved into the hilltop one level below. Functionality and energy efficiency are achieved both by this programmatic zoning, which allows the lower level to be shut down during periods when there are no guests. The efficiencies of the layout are supplemented by careful choice of materials, fixtures, fittings, and energy systems. The 'greening' of the house complements its visual warmth, grounding the modern structure in its rural landscape.

Building systems include the use of a geothermal field that greatly reduces energy consumption and costs associated with heating and cooling of the house. The house also has a rainwater collection system that collects 80 percent of water that falls on the rooftops and re-uses it for both toilets and landscaping needs. A green roof is incorporated over the guest wing to reduce water run-off and provide high insulation values. Structural systems include a poured-in-place concrete lower level, with steel frame upper level super structure complemented by traditional wood framing throughout.

Materials include corten steel entry façade, cumaru wood siding, decks and interior floors, painted and stained oak and birch veneer cabinetry. All window systems and appliances and building system equipment are energy-star rated and lighting includes energy-efficient LED, fluorescent and low-voltage lighting throughout.

Photography by Daniel Levin

The green roof enhances the vistas from the upper level

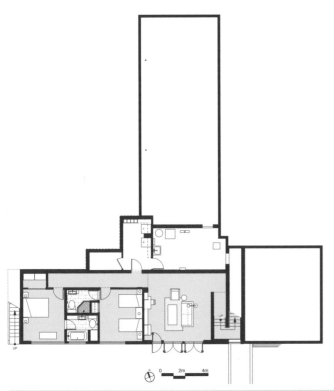

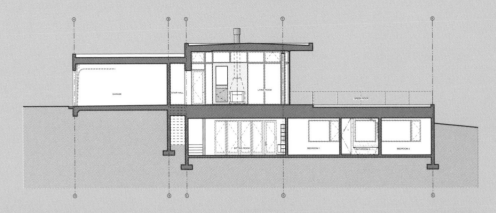

Villa Decanes was built in León, Spain, for a wine-maker family. For its construction, the architects at **Alarcón + Asociados** used pavilions to interconnect the house, inspired by the style used in the Chinese traditional architecture of the Unesco World Heritage listed Gardens of Suzhou. This self-assembly method is low-cost at only half the usual price, less than €400 per square metre (US$50 per square foot).

The structure consists of load-bearing walls made out of lightened clay that provide the house with thermal insulation. The beam system – made of precast concrete and clay – comprises 5-metre (16-foot) spans and supports the habitable green roof. Thanks to the roof's soil and vegetation, not only does it provide insulation and thermal inertia, but it also absorbs solar radiation.

The house is heated with a low-temperature radiant floor connected to solar panels during the winter. In summer it is cooled with cross ventilation during the night and blinds controlling solar radiation during the day (as per traditional Spanish architecture).

The different levels of the slab define diverse scale spaces, as well as the connection between interior levels. The horizontal connection of spaces is achieved through diagonal alignment of pavilions and axial continuity of doors.

Photography by Alberto Alarcón, Pablo Cruz

The clients adapted the house geometry to suit their own needs and gradual colonisation of the space

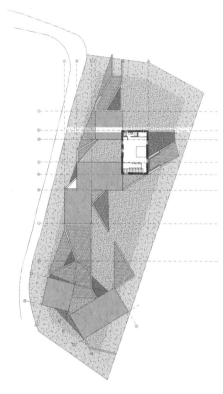

REFLECTING OUT TO SEA

Overlooking the Pacific Ocean in Sydney, Australia, **Seacliff House** incorporates two green roofs – one at the roof level and another at ground level above a basement garage.

The house was planned on four levels. **Chris Elliott Architects** conceived the basement level as a watery grotto. The sandstone is carved away to create space. This connects in an intimate way the house to the very essence of Sydney – its sandstone base. Water occurs at various levels – a pool, a shallow reflecting pool with a bridge and an outside bath. At times strong shafts of light penetrate the spaces, as through rock fissures in a cave. At other times when light levels are low strong colours help to create warmth and atmosphere.

At the entry to the house there is a beautiful aquatic roof garden that was designed by the landscape architect Vladimir Sitta, a good friend of the architect. It consists of a series of granite slabs forming a bridge across a shallow pond containing small fish. The fish can be seen through brass frames that act as 'windows' into the water. Water trickles from slots carved into two of the stone slabs. The surface of the water is covered with aquatic plants, such as duckweed and floating ferns, forming a kind of large green abstract canvas.

Envisaged as a belvedere (a structure built in an elevated position to provide lighting and ventilation and to command a fine view) or lookout, a rooftop study opens onto a small sundeck. Here there are panoramic views over the ocean.

A private sundeck with built in timber seating and a fireplace provides a comfortable place to contemplate the ocean and the stars at night.

Around the outside of this curved white element, the roof area is working very hard to incorporate a range of sustainable elements: solar panels, skylights and water collection. In between these elements, the remaining areas are covered with plantings of pigface, a native coastal succulent that blooms with beautiful pink flowers in early summer. This plant provides excellent thermal insulation for the roof of the house and creates an intriguing green drapery as it hangs over the sides, replicating the pigface in the wild's habit across the natural rock shelf below.

Photography by Chris Elliott, Richard Glover, Vladimir Sitta

Pigface retains its lush green colour throughout the year

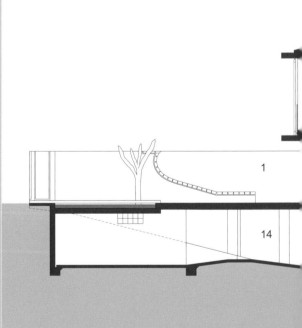

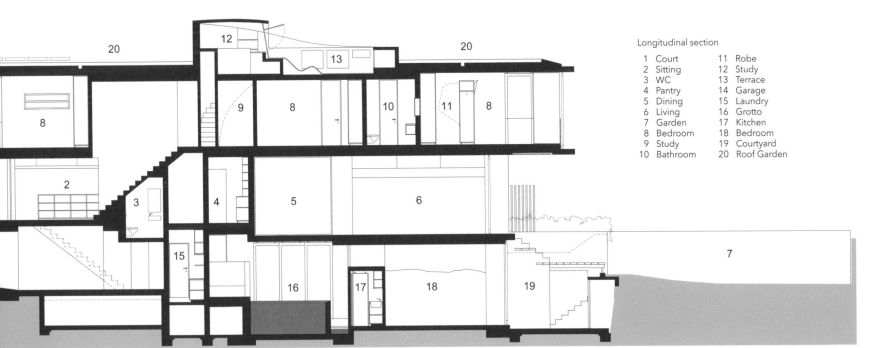

Longitudinal section

1	Court	11	Robe
2	Sitting	12	Study
3	WC	13	Terrace
4	Pantry	14	Garage
5	Dining	15	Laundry
6	Living	16	Grotto
7	Garden	17	Kitchen
8	Bedroom	18	Bedroom
9	Study	19	Courtyard
10	Bathroom	20	Roof Garden

SATURATING WITH SUNLIGHT

Melbourne is predominantly flat. There is no landscape to confine, therefore the building is free to become landscape. Hill House, by **Andrew Maynard Architects**, is a response to this possibility.

The thin allotments that dominate Melbourne's northern suburbs often provide indomitable constraints to solar access and therefore require the production of unorthodox ideas to overcome these constraints and convert them into opportunities.

Hill House is a deliberate attempt to avoid any aestheticising of the project's sustainable credentials. Following the decision to build at the rear of the block a ubiquitous modern box was first imagined. Soon it seemed necessary to pursue the opportunity to activate this new, once shaded, now sunny façade: a seat along the new northern façade? Perhaps a series of steps like the Scalinata della Trinità dei Monti? But how does one lounge in the sun on steps. Perhaps a slope instead – and the Hill House emerged.

The new structure faces the Australian sun, employing passive solar gain and saturates itself with sunlight. Strategically the architectural celebration of the pure cantilevered form acts pragmatically as the passive solar eave to the outdoor space below, cutting out summer sun, while letting winter sun flood in.

Steel not only provides a solution for the architectural form explored, it is also the primary celebrated material within the small strategic palette applied. Steel has been celebrated as both a structural solution and an aesthetic: the black monolith is a continuous, full height steel truss. The monolith cantilevers more than it is grounded in the hill.

The benefit of the structure being in the backyard is that it borrows landscaping from its neighbours' gardens. Inside, the high windows about the entertainment cabinetry and the dining area are enveloped in trees. Internally, one gets the sense that Hill House is enveloped by bush, rather than forming part of the suburban mix.

Long strips of windows to the east and west have been equipped with operable louvres. The north-facing façade consists of an entire wall of the same mechanically operated louvres, providing the option of controlling cross-winds and sunlight.

The yard is water efficient – the use of synthetic grass, with strategically placed garden patches, create dense areas of planting, resulting in very little demand for water.

The grass on the hill envelops the ground floor in an additional layer of insulation; it is a thermal roof blanket, installed to supplement the existing insulation of the building structure beneath while also protecting the roof membrane.

Photography by Peter Bennetts, Nic Granleese

Hill House *is a simulacrum of an undulating landscape and the pure architectural form*

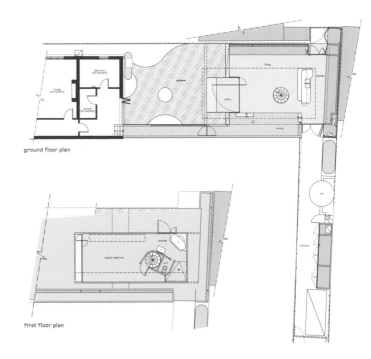

ground floor plan

first floor plan

SKIRTING WITH DESIGN

A family with one child (and possibly more to come) dreams of moving from their apartment in the middle of the city in Vienna, Austria, to a house at the urban periphery with plenty of green. They envision children playing in the grass, with the parents and their friends sitting among them, and all around there is nothing but green, trees, pure nature.

Caramel Architekten have transformed a 500-square-metre (5382-square-foot) plot in Vienna, Austria, that was a grassy meadow with trees into **500m² wohnzimmer** – a multilevel residence featuring a simple backyard complete with a pool.

The structure features four levels: three above-ground and one below, yielding a total of 300 square metres (3229 square feet) of living space. In order to retain the character of the original meadow, the ground-floor living and dining areas are tied to the garden in a generous sweeping gesture, displaying a curved geometry. The living room is composed of indoor and outdoor spaces that connect the house to its surroundings. The tail end of the swoosh tapers to human scale, forming smooth shallow depressions for sitting, curvilinear furniture, a pool and a terrace with rounded corners.

The sweeping gesture on the ground floor is made of semitransparent polycarbonate elements; the texture of these materials creates an ephemeral character to the building's design. The materials are also employed in the façade of the top floor, giving it the appearance of an airy, hovering swoosh, which makes the upper level appear to float above the backyard.

On the rooftop, the patch of meadow that was removed from the garden to build the house has been woven into the undulating green office landscape.

Photography by Hertha Hurnaus

The grassy green fields on several levels are interspersed with ephemeral swooshes of space

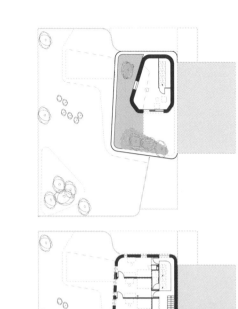

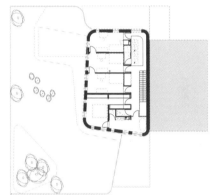

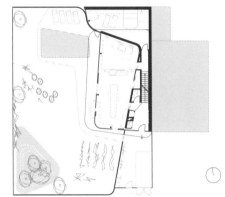

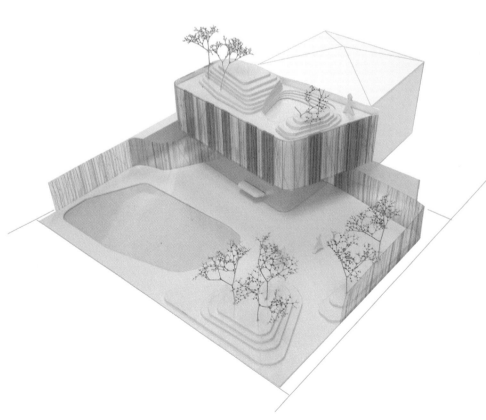

SUBVERTING THE LANDSCAPE

Taking its cues from both persona and place, **John Senhauser Architects** sought to reconcile a steeply sloped, wooded site with a livable log home in the woods. The **Walnut Woods** residence, situated in Ohio, USA, was conceived as a 45-metres-long by 7.3-metres-wide (24 feet by 150 feet) linear bar rising into the trees from northwest to southeast. Positioned according to subdivision covenants, the structure bridges 12 metres (40 feet) across an existing intermittent creek, thereby preserving the natural drainage patterns and habitat. The walnut trees, cleared from the site during construction, were locally milled and returned to the residence as hardwood flooring.

Drawing on the filtered light of a wooded presence, a 24.3-metre-long (80 feet) 'grand terrace' and double-height window wall were incised into the linear bar, dematerialising the heavy, log wall. The terrace provides sheltered entertaining space that is accessible from the primary living spaces, including kitchen, living and dining areas and master bedroom. Running the length of the terrace on the northeast elevation, the window wall not only provides continual connection to the surrounding woods, but it also enables indirect daylight to penetrate the interior, which minimises the need for artificial lighting. The structure's section rises successively up a cascading stair to culminate in a glass-enclosed meditative space (known lovingly as the 'bird feeder'), providing access to the grass roof via an exterior stair. The roof is planted with native grasses, laid out in a pattern dictated by the structural grid of the house.

Photography by Eric Williams, Scott Hisey

In a wealthy, suburban community characterised by large Georgian-style houses sitting on three-acre lawns, the rooftop lawn becomes subversive

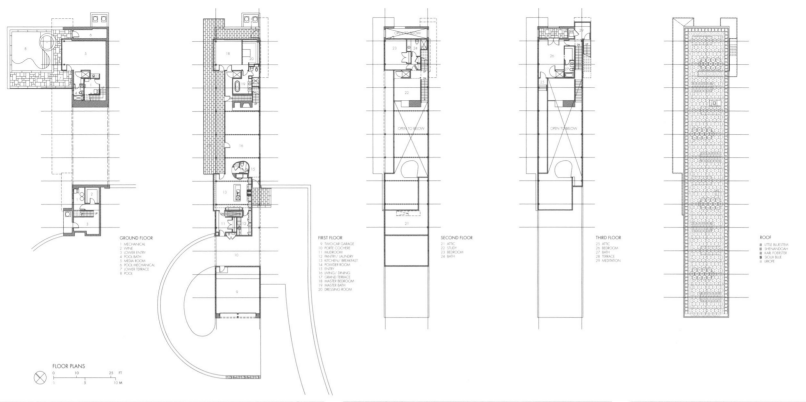

FLOOR PLANS

0   10   25 FT
0   5   10 M

GROUND FLOOR
1 MECHANICAL
2 WINE
3 LOWER ENTRY
4 POOL BATH
5 MEDIA ROOM
6 POOL MECHANICAL
7 LOWER TERRACE
8 POOL

FIRST FLOOR
9 TWO-CAR GARAGE
10 PORTE COCHERE
11 MUDROOM
12 PANTRY / LAUNDRY
13 KITCHEN / BREAKFAST
14 POWDER ROOM
15 ENTRY
16 LIVING / DINING
17 GRAND TERRACE
18 MASTER BEDROOM
19 MASTER BATH
20 DRESSING ROOM

SECOND FLOOR
21 ATTIC
22 STUDY
23 BEDROOM
24 BATH

THIRD FLOOR
25 ATTIC
26 BEDROOM
27 BATH
28 TERRACE
29 MEDITATION

ROOF
LITTLE BLUESTEM
SHENANDOAH
KARL FOERSTER
SIOUX BLUE
LIRIOPE

TAKING TO THE HILLS

The **8 House** sits on the outer edge of the city as the southern most outpost of Orestad in Copenhagen, Denmark. The bow-tie-shaped 61,000-square-metre (656,598 square feet) mixed-use building comprises three different types of residential housing and 10,000 square metres (107,639 square feet) of retail spaces and offices. Rather than a traditional block, the 8 House stacks all the ingredients of a lively urban neighbourhood into horizontal layers of typologies, connected by a continuous promenade and cycling path up to the 10th floor, creating a three-dimensional urban neighborhood – where suburban life merges with the energy of a big city, where business and housing co-exist.

BIG CPH has created two intimate interior courtyards, separated by the centre of the cross, which houses 500 square metres (5,381 square feet) of communal facilities available to all residents. At the very same spot, the building is penetrated by a 9-metre-wide (29 feet) passage that allows people to easily move from the park area on its western edge to the water-filled canals to the east. Instead of dividing the different functions of the building – for both habitation and trade – into separate blocks, the various functions are spread out horizontally.

The apartments are placed at the top while the commercial program unfolds at the base of the building. As a result, the different horizontal layers achieve a quality of their own: the apartments

benefit from the view, sunlight and fresh air, while the office leases merge with life on the street. This layering is emphasized by the shape of 8 House: it's hoisted up in the northeast corner and pushed down at the southwest corner, allowing light and air to enter the southern courtyard. This is an example of architectural alchemy – the mix allows the individual activities to find their way to the most ideal location within the common framework – the retail facing street, the offices towards northern light and the residences with sun and views to the open spaces.

A continuous public path stretches from street level to the penthouses and allows people to bike all the way from the ground floor to the top, moving alongside townhouses with terraced gardens, winding through an urban perimeter block.

The 8 House uses size to its advantage by creating immense differences in height, thereby creating a unique sense of community with small gardens and pathways that resemble the intimacy of an Italian hill town, with spectacular views towards the Copenhagen Canal and Kalvebod Faelled's protected open spaces.

Two sloping green roofs totalling 1,700 square metres (18,299 square feet) are strategically placed to reduce the urban heat island effect, and provide the visual identity to the project and tie it back to the adjacent farmlands towards the south.

8 House is a three-dimensional neighbourhood rather than an architectural object

Photography by Jens Lindhe, Dragor Luftfoto, Jan Magasanik, Jesper Ray, Urik Reeh, Ty Stange, Bjarne Tulinius

GLOSSARY OF TERMS

BIPV   building integrated photovoltaic

EPDM   ethylene propylene diene terpolymer

IPCC   intergovernmental panel on climate change

LED   light-emitting diode

LEED   leadership in energy & environmental design

OSB   oriented strand board

PET   polyethylene terephthalate

INDEX